Cowtown Carving

by

Stephen H. Prescott

Fox Chapel Publishing
Box 7948
Lancaster, PA 17604

This is the second revised edition of Cowtown Carving incorporating new half-tone photograph reproductions. Originally self-published, this edition is published by Fox Chapel Publishing Co. Inc.

Illustrated by: Stephen H. Prescott and Herbert Kaminski Crivitz, Wisconsin
Photography by: Stephen H. Prescott and Ronnie & Vaudine Dulin Lubbock, Texas
Introduction by: David M. Dunham, DDS, MSD, Cleburne, Texas

Manufactured in the United States of America

ISBN#1-56523-049-3

To order additional copies of this book,
please send $14.95 and $2.00 to:

Fox Chapel Publishing
Book Orders
Box 7948
Lancaster, PA 17604-7948

Please try your favorite book supplier first!

CONTENTS

Preface   Preface 3

Introduction   Introduction 4

Acknowledgements   Acknowledgements 5

Chapters   Chapter 1 ● Woods, Tools and Sharpening 7
              Chapter 2 ● Carving Faces 9
              Chapter 3 ● Carving Eyes 13
              Chapter 4 ● Carving Hands 17
              Chapter 5 ● Painting, Antiquing, Finishing 21
              Chapter 6 ● Caricature Ideas, Tips and Not So Secret Secrets . . . 25
              Chapter 7 ● Read More About It 29
              Chapter 8 ● Projects 1-15 31

Projects   Project 1 ● Confused Cowboy 33
              Project 2 ● Cowboy P.H.D. (Post Hole Digger) 35
              Project 3 ● "Rummy" Belcher, Town Drunk 37
              Project 4 ● "Ricky Wreck," the Rank Bull Rider 39
              Project 5 ● The Cowboy Cowboy Carver 41
              Project 6 ● Cowtown Santa 43
              Project 7 ● Doc Croakum 45
              Project 8 ● Digger Dirge, the Undertaker 47
              Project 9 ● "Bronc-itis" 49
              Project 10 ● Shady Schyster -- Lawyer of Cheatum, Crook,
                            Pettifogger and Schyster 51
              Project 11 ● Brother Paul, the Circuit Riding Preacher 53
              Project 12 ● Sage Soliloquy, Town Philosopher 55
              Project 13 ● Bad Dude Bandit 57
              Project 14 ● The Tailgater 59
              Project 15 ● Slug Hazard, Rodeo Clown 61

Chapter   Chapter 9 ● Patterns and Line Drawings for Projects 63

Afterword   Afterword 95

PREFACE

Why another cowboy caricature carving book? What can I say that hasn't already been said by well known caricature carver/authors such as Harold Enlow or Claude Bolton? What niche can I fill? These are questions I've asked myself as friends, students, and loved ones have encouraged me to write a book. I don't want to rehash the same old cowboy subjects or the same materials covered by others. You will not find in this book detailed sections on selection of wood, selection and use of tools, or how to sharpen them. These subjects have already been effectively covered by the aforementioned authors (see Chapter 7). I will assume that you have your favorite wood and tools and can sharpen them, that you are experienced enough to "move some wood", and that you can shape a body with a pattern and general instructions. I have found that most of my carving students have the greatest difficulties in carving faces, eyes, and hands. It is these areas that I want to address. In addition, I hope you'll find some different, fun patterns and some new ideas to add character to your caricatures. These projects are aimed at the intermediate carver who is seeking some new challenges and ideas to stimulate his or her carving skills.

The chapter on Caricature Ideas is designed to give you ideas to customize your carvings. Use my basic patterns, but add or delete to give it your own personal touch. Modify the patterns to suit your needs. Most of the body patterns are 3x3x8 and head patterns 3x3x3 but with most modern copy machines you can easily enlarge or reduce as needed.

Fort Worth, "Where the West Begins", is a great place to find subject material for the cowboy caricature carver, especially in the Fort Worth Stockyards. In the stockyards you will find cowboys, young and old, rich and broke, all duded up or filthy from honest cowboy work. It's an area that draws real cowboys, would-be cowboys (Rexall Rangers), and tourists with such attractions as the world's largest honky tonk, Billy Bob's Texas, and the White Elephant Saloon. It also has an indoor rodeo (first of its kind), nationally known restaurants, and local greasy spoon cafes. There are art galleries and museums featuring fine western art. There is even Cowboy Church to minister to the spiritual needs of this unique community. Throw in the annual celebrations of Pioneer Days and the Chisholm Trail Roundup, and you'll find a never ending source of ideas and models of old traditional cowboys, contemporary western styles, and typical western tourists. I had a small carving shop in the stockyards for about a year. On a daily basis I had the opportunity to observe a variety of western culture in this unique setting. Most of my cowboy caricature carvings are modeled after characters found in the stockyards. Since I find most single carvings boring, I like to display mine in small humorous scenes that show a small piece of cowboy life. The situations that are common to cowboys are better laughed at than cried about. I hope that you'll see humor and enjoy them as much as I have.

INTRODUCTION

From the opening paragraph to the final word, Tom Clancy's novels grasp your attention with the intensity of a steel trap. There is no excess baggage -- each word and phrase is essential -- concise, compact, and unified in the telling of a tale.

Steve Prescott has captured the essence of caricature carving as Clancy has seized the essentials of the action novel. Steve's carvings achieve all the goals of excellent caricature by their streamlined style, unified point of view, and directness in the telling of a story. "*COWTOWN CARVING*" could well be the Bible of caricature, and those who carve in this style would do well to study this book -- not just the precision of the carving, but the thought and purpose that has gone into the creation of the figures and scenes as each reveals its story.

It has been said by the ignorant and/or untalented that a caricature is a realistic carving that went bad. Those who know better realize that a good caricature exhibits as stringent a discipline as good realism. The caricaturist must first know what is normal, then be able to identify those features that deviate from the average and thus give the subject its individuality. By isolation and exaggeration of these identifying features, the caricaturist is then able to convey the point of the story to the viewer.

In my early woodcarving endeavors, I had the opportunity to attend one of Steve's Labor Day Seminars, and I was hooked. The cleanliness of the carving, the story-telling effects of expression and movement, and the elimination of nonessential detail struck a chord in my soul for the love of a good short story. I've been trying to capture that vitality ever since.

Steve's teaching background, his sense of humor, his appreciation for the frailties of human nature, and his holistic approach to the art of woodcarving particularly qualify him as a unique caricature artist. One could do a lot worse in emulating the style and philosophy of Steve Prescott.

David M. Dunham, DDS, MSD
President-Affiliated Woodcarvers, LTD
Secretary-Caricature Carvers of America
1992 Texas Whittling Champion

ACKNOWLEDGMENTS

It's nearly impossible to remember all who have influenced me as a carver and helped me with this book. Trying to list them all, much less thank them all, will in doubt offend all those that I forget, but I will risk their ire and beg their forgiveness.

Within a fifty mile radius of Fort Worth, we have some of this country's best caricature carvers. I admit to being prejudiced. The competition, encouragement, and camaraderie of such outstanding caricature carvers as Claude Bolton, Gary Batte, Dave Dunham, Chris Hammack, Jack Price and Charlie Winstead have all been a positive influence on me for which I am very grateful.

Members of the Fort Worth Woodcarvers Club and Texas Woodcarvers Guild such as Derald, Johnny, J. L., Royce, Rex, Frank, Les, Jim, Ron, Ivan and Trudy have all at different times and in their own individual ways encouraged and supported my efforts.

A special thanks to my longtime friends Ronnie and Vaudine Dulin for their photographic advice and help in this book. Thanks also to Herb Kaminski, one of my former students, a professional technical illustrator who insisted that my bandsaw patterns should be accompanied by line drawings and volunteered his services to draw them.

You will notice that under the heading of each project are names of collectors and friends who have purchased the original carving projects in this book. Their support and patience while waiting for me to complete this book have helped make this endeavor a little easier. I thank you.

I would be remiss not to mention my mom and dad who have been a constant source of encouragement. Mom kind of pushed me into carving by insisting that I do something with the talent she knew was there. Of course, "every mama crow thinks her baby is the blackest". Their talents and interests as an artist and as a woodworker have certainly been passed on to their first born and his siblings.

How can I thank the one person who has always thought everything I carved was a masterpiece? At least she never let on otherwise. My wife, Pat, who has also been my best friend for twenty years, has been my strongest supporter, advisor, salesman, and organizer. Those of you who know her know what an essential part of my classes she is. You also know that if you want something done its best to ask her rather than me. Her gentle prodding to get this book going and her work on the computer have made this book a reality.

CHAPTER 1
Woods, Tools and Sharpening

As I said in the preface, I feel that these subjects have been ably covered by others more qualified than I, and I will keep my comments to a minimum on these subjects.

Woods

While any wood can be carved, there are some woods that are better than others. I use basswood almost exclusively for my caricatures because of its nice even texture, its detail holding abilities, and little or no grain pattern. Since I paint most of my caricatures, the last trait is no problem. It would be sacrilegious to paint over such beautiful woods as walnut, butternut, or catalpa. Northern basswood, kiln dried is preferred. Other woods suitable for caricature carving are: jelutong, sugar pine, tupelo, white pine, aspen, and cottonwood. I'm sure there are others that may be available to you locally. Of course, the best wood for carving is free wood.

Tools

As in any hobby, carvers tend to accumulate more tools than they need. If I had a line of tools to sell I might recommend specific tools necessary to make certain cuts more easily. I have found that it is not so much the tool that one uses as it is the one using the tool with skill that makes a good carving. The longer I carve, the fewer tools I tend to use. Having given you that bit of un-solicited philosophy, I hope that you never try to carry my tool box.

Most of the carvings in this book can be executed with the following sharp tools:

Bench knife
Small v-tool
1/4"-3/8" 60 degree v-tool
3/16" veiner
1/4"-3/4" gouge

These are also what I recommend for beginners in caricature carving.

Sharpening

I once heard a well known carver respond when questioned about the single most important trait necessary to become a good carver. After thinking for a while he replied "The ability to sharpen." At first that evaluation seemed a bit odd, but I now realize that he was probably correct. You cannot carve effectively and enjoyably unless you learn to sharpen. Unfortunately, it is dirty, boring, and time consuming. Most of us just don't want to invest the time and effort necessary to develop the skills to sharpen effectively. I am convinced that there are as many different methods to sharpen as there are carvers. My advice is to find a way that works for you and stick with it. Changing methods often prevents one from perfecting sharpening skills.

If you are still struggling with sharpening I would highly recommend any of Harold Enlow's carving books. Each book has an excellent section on sharpening knives, chisels, gouges, and v-tools with simple, easy to follow instructions.

CHAPTER 2
Carving Faces

To my way of thinking, the face (expression) is everything in caricature carving. I have often said to my students that I am not too concerned about carving detailed ears on my pieces (except for competition). If someone who views my carving starts examining the ears instead of focusing on the face, then I've lost them anyway and that piece probably should be considered a failure. If you want to be a successful caricature carver, it is essential that you master face carving skills.

We will not concentrate here on proportions or learning to carve specific expressions. This has already been covered in books such as *Learn to Carve Faces and Expressions* by Harold L. Enlow, or Claude W. Bolton's *Carving Heads, Hats and Hair*. I especially encourage you to examine Jack Hamm's *Cartooning the Head and Figure*. It is an excellent source for different facial expressions. On pages 19 to 23, Hamm shows 150 expressions alphabetically arranged from aggressive to zealous. As novice carvers we were all ecstatic just to get recognizable eyes, mouths, and noses on the correct side of the head. As we grow as caricature carvers, we should be able to convey a message through expressions without words to explain the piece. Use of Hamm's book has helped me in this progression and I urge you to add it to your library if you are serious about being a good caricature carver.

Books can serve as valuable aids by helping us to more precisely craft our pieces. However, books alone cannot help us become proficient at caricature carving.

There is no substitute for practice in learning to carve faces. You will always be tense and apprehensive until you have "paid your dues" by building skill and confidence on something other than your finished piece. I use practice sticks approximately 2x2x12 to improve my face carving skills. The sticks are saved for future reference. We will use one of these progression face sticks to demonstrate how to set up and carve a face.

Mark your practice stick into 4 equal segments on each side. Three inches each is about right. Next, place marks on opposite corners of the stick for the bridge-eye groove notch and the base of the nose-oral mound notch. These marks will be approximately one third of each segment. You should now have the stick prepared to carve eight faces, four on each opposite side.

Step 1 - Facial Planes (Fig. 1A and 1B)
Begin to establish the facial planes by making a stop-cut at the bridge of the nose. This cut is almost parallel to the surface of the wood. The second cut begins at the tip of the nose up to the first stop-cut. Repeat this cut until you get the desired depth. This forms the top ridge of the nose. The next two sets of planes are on both sides of the nose. These cuts are almost in identical planes to the first cuts and form the cheeks and eye sockets.

Form the notch under the nose by cutting in nearly perpendicular to the surface and removing the wood a little at a time until you achieve the desired depth under the nose. Be sure to make the perpendicular stop-cut first, or the face will be noseless

Progression Step
Face Stick

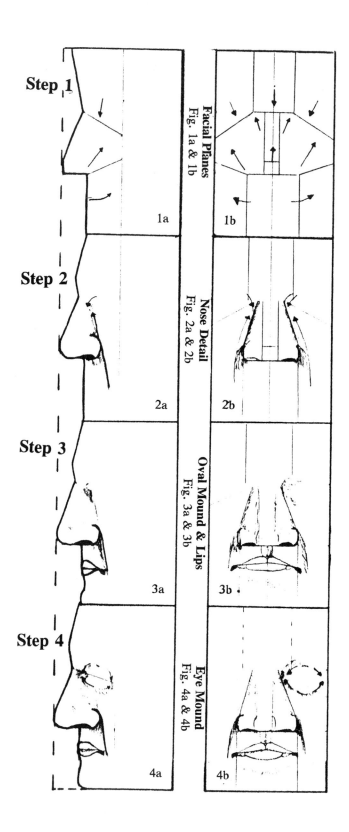

Step 1

Facial Planes
Fig. 1a & 1b

1a   1b

Step 2

Nose Detail
Fig. 2a & 2b

2a   2b

Step 3

Oval Mound & Lips
Fig. 3a & 3b

3a   3b

Step 4

Eye Mound
Fig. 4a & 4b

4a   4b

and you'll have to start all over again. This is a point at which many carvers stop and create problems later. Observe that the nose is as much into the face as out of the face. In other words, the distance from the tip of the nose to the base of the nose is about equal to the distance from the base of the nose to the back edge of the wing, into the face. The oral mound below the nose must be rounded here to avoid having the whole nose sitting on the outside of the face which is very typical of most novice carvings.

With the completion of these cuts, the planes of the face should now be obvious from both the front and in the profile. The best way to learn this step is to repeat it right on down the practice stick seven more times until it becomes automatic to set up a face this way. We are now ready to move on to Step 2.

Step 2 - Nose Detail (Fig. 2A and 2B)
In this step we will form the nose pyramid, wings, nostrils, and set the smile line. Begin by determining the desired width of the nose. Leave the bridge of the nose wide at this point since it will narrow as the nose develops. Using a 3/16" veiner, make a stop cut by guiding the veiner across, down, and into the inside corner of the eye. Guide the veiner from the base of the nose upward to the stop-cut at the inside corner of the eye. Be careful to remove the wood from the cheek side rather than the nose side or the bridge will become too narrow. Several passes may be necessary to get depth into the corner. Use a knife to blend from the top ridge of the nose into the groove and thereby form a pyramid with a flat top.

Deepen the wing position by removing a triangular chip from the area where the smile lines joins the nose wing. This will help bring the nose farther into the face. Use a 1/4" half round gouge to form the wing. Shape the wing with your knife. The wing can also be set in with a knife or v-tool. Form the nostrils with a knife or gouge. Be careful not to force the cut and break the wing. Repeat Step 2 seven times down the practice stick.

Step 3 - Oral Mound and Lips (Fig. 3A and 3B)
Establish the smile line, from the top of the wing downward, using a knife or v-tool. Round and blend the mound into the smile line. The oral mound should now be formed. The mouth is easily carved if you think of it as being five distinct planes: two upper planes, one large lower plane with two small outside planes. Blend these planes as necessary. The mouth should have an end at each corner. Create a shadow by removing a small triangle from each corner. Use the 1/4" half round gouge to create a groove between the lower lip and chin. Carve the philtrum from the upper lip to the base of the nose using the same gouge. Repeat this step six times down the practice stick.

Step 4 - Eye Mound (Fig. 4A and 4B)
Use the 3/16" veiner to relieve wood to form an eye mound. Round and smooth the mound to look as if the eye were closed.

Remember that the eye is actually an eyeball protected by bones, surrounded and supported by muscles and flesh. This mound is curved equally from top to bottom and side to side. Inside and outside corners should be about the same depth. When viewed in profile, the lower lid is recessed into the face a little deeper than is the upper. Try to achieve a sleeping or closed eye effect. Repeat this step five times down the practice stick. Carving the eye itself will be in Chapter 3.

Step 5 - Brow Ridge and Eyebrows
All of the projects in this book are males and the brow ridge on the masculine face is much more prominent than on the female. To accent (caricature) this feature use a 3/16" veiner or 1/4" gouge to re-move wood between the eyes. Begin at the bridge and push the gouge upward to the hat or hairline. Several passes may be necessary depending on the expression you want to achieve.

The next step is to remove wood above the eyebrow using your thin-bladed knife. A rolling motion from the top of the eyebrow upward to the hairline should establish the forehead while leaving a brow ridge on which you will carve hair for the eyebrow. Without leaving wood for the brow ridge, the eyebrow hair must be carved into the forehead, which is the opposite of what you want.

You are now ready to add the hair for the eyebrows. Use a sharp, small v-tool or a small veiner to texture the hair. The small v-tool tends to tear or chip, especially going cross grain, even when very sharp. I prefer to use the small (1 or 2 mm) veiner because it doesn't have this tendency. Short irregular strokes, overlapping but not criss-crossing, give the best effect.

Don't worry too much about the length of the hair because the eyebrow can be trimmed later using the thin-bladed knife with the previously used roll cut. Repeat this step four times down the practice stick.

You should now be getting very familiar with the face stick and understand how to set up a face fairly quickly. By way of review, we began by (1) setting up the facial planes, (2) adding nose detail, (3) forming the oral mound and the lips, (4) preparing the eye mound and finally, (5) adding detail to the brow ridge and eyebrows. You will note that you should have three almost identical faces without eyes. We will remedy this situation in Chapter 3, Carving Eyes.

CHAPTER 3
Carving Eyes

As stated earlier, since caricature is the deliberate exaggeration or distortion of realism, it is important that the caricaturist have a good knowledge of human anatomy. It is with this premise in mind that we will make note of a few general observations about human eye structure.

General Observations
Remember, as stated in Chapter 2, Step 4, the eye is actually a ball surrounded and supported by bone and tissue. Only about 20% of the eyeball is visible between the eyelids. The eyeball continues the same curvature under the bone and flesh and should not be carved with abrupt drops at each corner. Neither should the eyelid be outlined deeply with your knife tip since the eyeball should appear to continue its curve under the upper and lower lids. When viewed in profile, only the outside half of the eyeball should be visible. If the eyemound is set up properly, the correct eye curvature is much more likely to be carved.

I find it much easier to carve two similar eyes if I carve both eyes simultaneously alternating steps between the right and left eyes until both are completed together. In seminars, it is common for the instructor to demonstrate carving one eye, then return the carving to the student to duplicate. (My students complain that I always carve the easy one, usually the right). The student often struggles in vain and marvels at the expertise of the instructor who made it look so easy. In reality, most instructors could not exactly duplicate an eye that the student had carved either. Try developing both eyes at the same time if you find it difficult to get them carved similarly.

The lower eyelid does not move except when pushed upward by the cheeks. The upper lid moves thereby creating different expressions. The level of the inner and outside corners of the eye is different in women and children than it is in men. In women and children, the level of the curved lower lid seems to be slightly upward on the outside corner. Women even apply their makeup to accent this characteristic. The lower lid on men, especially older, weathered men, is lower on the outside corner. In carving caricature cowboys, I like to exaggerate this characteristic which makes them look older, tired and worn.

A common mistake is to try to show too much of the iris (colored part of the eye). Showing all of the iris will give the figure a very unnatural, bug-eyed look. The upper and lower eyelids usually cover part of the iris at all times. Observe some eyes in closeup photographs in a magazine and you'll soon understand what I'm saying.

Tools
All tools must be very sharp to carve the eyes effectively. We frequently carve the eyes last, after hours of work. The tools at this point are not their sharpest, and the results are often disappointing. Take the extra time to buff or sharpen. It will pay off with more pleasing results. A sharp thin-pointed knife, a small veiner, and a small v-tool are usually all the tools you will need to carve the caricature eyes that will be demonstrated here.

Step 6 - Eyes
Step 6 continues your face stick from Chapter 2. You should have three faces

Regular Eye

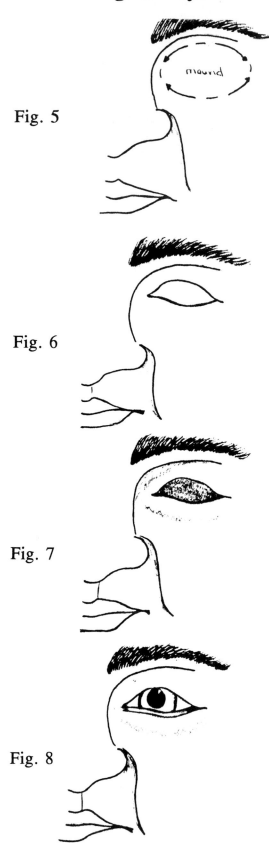

Fig. 5

Fig. 6

Fig. 7

Fig. 8

left to carve several different types of eyes. Three types of eyes will be explained here, the regular eye, the old, bagged eye, and the cartoon eye.

The Regular Eye (Fig. 5, 6, 7, 8) -- This is the standard eye that most people carve. Some instructors use different tools or methods, with some variation, although it still is the same basic eye in the end.

Begin by marking the inside corners of each eye, then the outside corners. Be sure that the marks are equally balanced. The outside corner usually looks better if it is slightly lower than the inside corner. Next draw in the lower eyelid line (Fig. 5). This line is only slightly curved since the lower lid is almost stationary. Mark the upper lid line with the desired amount of opening needed for the expression you want.

Begin carving the eye by lightly scoring the upper and lower lid lines with your thin-bladed knife (Fig. 6). Many carvers make this line too deep and it creates problems later. If you have trouble with making this cut too deep, perhaps you would be better off using a small, <u>sharp</u> v-tool. Be sure to rotate the v-tool to the inside to remove wood from the eyeball side, not the lid side.

Using the thin-blade knife, slice wood from the sclera (white part of the eye)(Fig. 7). Be careful to maintain the same curve top to bottom and side to side. Do not deepen excessively at the corners. Remember: You are carving a ball covered by skin, and the ball should appear to continue under the skin. Slice the wood. Do not pry or pick at the wood since this will leave lots of fuzzies. If the slice does not pop out cleanly then rescore your stop cut. Repeat this process as many times as necessary until it looks the way you want it to look.

A crease in the upper lid may be added

especially to the inside corner to add more character (Fig. 8). Use a small v-tool or knife. The lower lid usually looks better with small shadow lines along its length, corner to corner. Be careful not to chip off the lower lid. Rotate the small v-tool downward to prevent chipping and crumbling of the lower lid.

The Old, Bagged Eye (Fig. 9, 10, 11, 12) -- This eye is a variation of the Regular Eye, but it does work well on ugly, well-worn, weathered cowboys. A fleshy sagging bag covers the upper outside lid, as well as a sagging lower eyelid and a bag under the eye. Approximately 1/2 to 2/3 of the iris and pupil will be visible, giving the eye a lazy, tired look.

To carve this eye, the eye mound (Step 4) should be modified to leave more wood at the upper outside corners (Fig. 9). This will leave enough material to form the upper sagging bag. Once the eye mound has been formed, draw in the sagging upper bag (Fig. 10). Cut a shallow line with the knife. This cut should be slightly deeper at the inside and outside corners as it follows the curve of the eyeball. Relieve the wood under the bag with the knife blade. Be careful to keep the eyeball rounded as it is easy to flatten the eye at this stage. Remember, the eye is a ball covered by skin. You may need to soften the edge of the upper bag by rounding it slightly with your knife.

You are now ready to draw in the upper and lower lid (Fig. 11). The upper lid will disappear under the bag leaving about 2/3 of the eyeball to carve. The rest of the eye is basically like the regular eye.

Cut a <u>shallow</u> line with the tip of the knife, following the lines drawn. Again, follow the curve of the eyeball with the line being a little deeper at the corners. Slice the wood from the eyeball itself. Do not pick it out -- this will leave "fuzzies". At this time you may need to remove

Old Bagged Eye

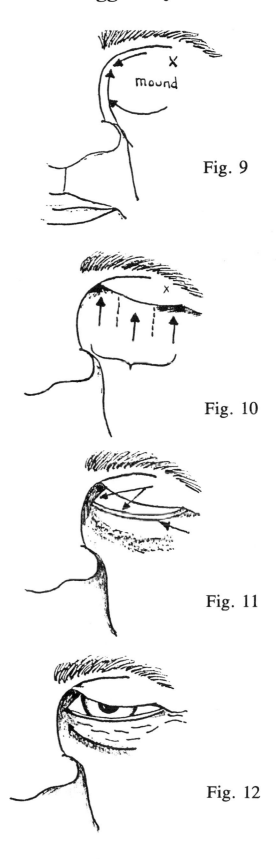

Fig. 9

Fig. 10

Fig. 11

Fig. 12

Some Cartoon Eye Possibilities   Fig. 13

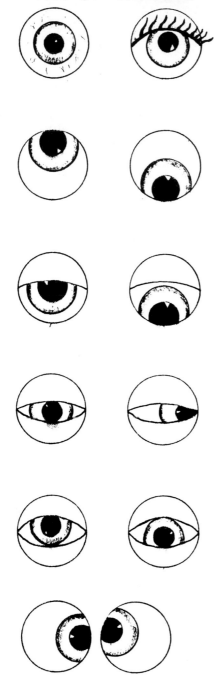

wood from the lower lid (Fig. 11). The lower lid should be recessed so that upper lid would close over the lower if the eye was closed. Using the <u>sharp</u> v-tool, carve a line just below the edge of the lower lid. Rotate the v-tool so that the wood is cut from the bottom of the v. If you don't cut it this way, the lid will usually tear or chip off. This cut can also be made with

a sharp knife if you prefer. Be sure that the outside edge of the lower lid goes under the sagging upper bag.

Now carve the bag under the eye using the veiner, v-tool, or knife, dependent upon your desired effect (Fig. 12). The sharper, deeper cuts would indicate more age and weathering. You may want to add more wrinkles with your sharp v-tool across the bag or add crow's feet at the outside corners.

The Cartoon Eye (Fig. 13) -- This eye is really quite versatile and very easy to carve once you get the hang of it. It works very well on animal caricatures as well. The cartoon eye is nothing more than a circle or oval with many variations.

To make the cartoon eye, draw the circle or oval first. Next, lightly outline the marks with your knife tip. Remove wood from the inside edge of the circle, leaving the center as the highest point. If you want the eyeball to bulge more, remove wood from the outside and repeat the whole process until you get the look you want. Lids can be easily added to change the expression. The circle can be modified to an oval vertically or horizontally or even diagonally. By experimenting on your practice stick you come up with even more variations. I have drawn some possibilities that you may want to try.

The carving of the different types of eyes brings us to the end of the progression face stick: Step 1 -- Facial planes, Step 2 -- Nose detail, Step 3 -- Oral mound and lips, Step 4 -- Eye mound, Step 5 -- Brow ridge and eyebrow, Step 6, 7, 8 -- Eyes. Again, there is no substitute for practice and for the confidence that comes with having put in the time to become proficient.

A cast study piece of this progression face stick is available from the author.

16

CHAPTER 4
Carving Hands

The carving of hands should be one of the easiest things we do as carvers since we ~~~~~~~~~~~~~~~~~ available

Caricature hands need to be exaggerated in size. The hand size from the butt of the palm to the tip of your longest finger is about equal to the size of the face from chin to hair. The exception to this rule is, of course, all of you with receding hairlines. Larger heads on caricatures would necessitate larger hands as well. Because this basic proportion is not understood, I often observe caricature cowboy carvings with hands that look too feminine. Carving a hand becomes easier if you block it in planes then add individual finger planes. I usually begin with the back of the hand, which is gauged by being one-half the size of the face. The back of the hand on these small caricatures can be carved in three planes. The first plane being from the middle knuckle to the last knuckle back to the wrist. This will leave a narrow, second flat plane between the index and middle knuckle as a transition plane. The third plane is triangular in shape and forms the webbing between the thumb and the index finger. It is most easily carved in one stroke by placing the knife blade across the knuckles, from the index finger to the thumb slicing back toward the wrist, removing the triangular chip. On small hands these planes are barely distinguishable, but understanding them will make your carvings more believable.

Next, determine the length for the fingers. Remember they are about equal to the hand length. Mark about half way for the first set of knuckles and half way for the remaining knuckle. The nailbed will be approximately half of the last finger section. If you make all of these marks at one time you'll just have to re-mark them.

6.   The fingernail is app   ne-half of the last knuckle.
7.   The little finger moves toward the center line of the palm when the hand is closed.
8.   The thumb length is about equal to the second knuckle of the index finger.
9.   When closed or clenched, the thumb locks over the middle finger to secure the grip.

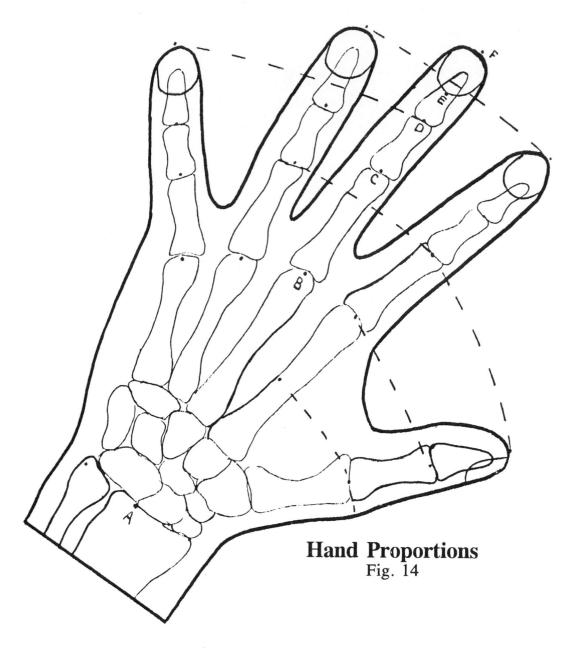

Hand Proportions
Fig. 14

Carve one set at a time then mark the next set. Once the basic hand and finger planes have been established, divide the hand for fingers. Draw the first line for the index and middle fingers slightly more than half way. Split each of these two about evenly to get four fingers. If you carve the divisions in one long stroke you'll destroy the finger planes you have worked to set up. Use a v-tool to divide the fingers. Carve each plane with individual cuts of the v-tool. If you carve the divisions in one long stroke you'll destroy the finger planes you have worked to set up.

Use your knife to deepen the cuts between the fingers, leaving the knuckles a little larger. Wrinkles in the fingers can be carved using a sharp v-tool -- it must be sharp since the knuckle wrinkles usually go across the grain. Finally, add the finger nail using the same v-tool.

In this text we will use three basic hand positions with some variations. Relaxed (Fig. 15), clenched or grasping (Fig. 16), and pointing (Fig. 17) are the basic positions we will use for the projects in this book.

Basic Hand Positions

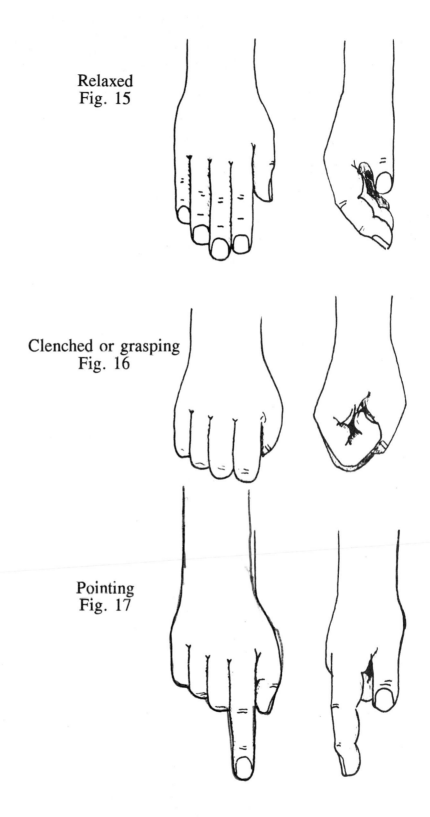

Relaxed
Fig. 15

Clenched or grasping
Fig. 16

Pointing
Fig. 17

"The prayer of a righteous man is powerful
and effective."

James 5:16

These hands of prayer may be seen in the Garden of Prayer, Church of Christ, North Richland Hills, Texas.

CHAPTER 5
Painting, Antiquing, Finishing

How you decide to finish your carving is a matter of personal taste. Most caricature carvings really seem to "come to life" when painted, which is what I prefer to do. Caricature carvings, when cleanly carved and full of character, can be very effectively finished using a natural sealer or stain. I've found no universal finishing technique; all have their good and bad points. In this chapter, I'll show several different methods of finishing. Experiment with each method until you get the effect that suits your individual tastes or needs.

Preparation

My first bit of advice on finishing is to wait. When I first began carving, I could hardly wait to paint and finish. As a result, many small details were unfinished and lots of little fuzzies were missed. Put up the "finished" carving for a few days. I am often amazed at the glaring mistakes that mysteriously appear when I set aside a carving. Sometimes we work so long and hard that we "can't see the forest for the trees". Give yourself a chance to produce your best work by being patient.

Secondly, your piece must be clean, free of oils and dirt. I assume that you had a mother who stressed hand hygiene; so I shouldn't have to lecture you on washing your hands to prevent your carving from being soiled by hand oils -- especially as the carving nears its final stages. If you didn't heed mother's good advice, the best way to remove hand oils and dirt from your carving is to use a good dishwashing liquid and a small amount of water. Do not soak the wood. Dry the carving thoroughly. A hair dryer can be used to speed up the process. Remove any fuzzies that may appear as the carving dries.

Painting

To my way of thinking, comparing unpainted to painted caricatures is like comparing the old black and white Betty Boop cartoons to *Who Framed Roger Rabbit*. Caricature carving is cartooning in wood and is greatly enhanced by color. You can use waterbased acrylics, watercolors, or artist's oils. All have their good points and bad. Regardless of what type of paint you choose, the most important thing is to use no more paint than is absolutely necessary. "THINK THIN." A slight suggestion of color is what you want, nothing more than a stain or wash. The wood grain must show through. Too much paint leaves a piece that looks like ceramic, plastic, or a cheap import.

My preference is waterbased acrylics because they are inexpensive, easy to mix and thin, dry quickly, have no odor, and easy to clean up. I have found Ceramcoat by Delta to be the best for my needs. They have a great variety of colors and the bottles are conveniently shaped so that you can squeeze out a small amount to thin with water. (A complete list of colors and numbers used on these projects is included at the end of Chapter 5). Ceramcoat also has the best flesh tones I've found. I never get the same colors twice when I've tried to mix a flesh color. I prefer to use thinned Ceramcoat Medium Flesh #2126 as a base fleshtone and then blend in Ceramcoat Caucasian Flesh #2029 as a highlighter on nose, cheeks, and lips. I use white full strength on eyes and teeth. Whites generally do not thin well with water. All other colors are thinned as much as possible to allow the wood grain to show through. Remember "THINK THIN."

One other bit of advice is not to skimp on paint brushes. A quality brush can make painting much more pleasurable and rewarding. Buy the best quality you can afford and clean it thoroughly when finished. A small amount of petroleum jelly is useful in reshaping and conditioning the bristles between uses.

Antiquing

The purpose of antiquing is to tone down the chalky, dried colors of water-thinned acrylic paint, to give the carving an earthy, subdued tone. It brings out the wood grain in the carving and highlights the clean tool marks. It also can hide a multitude of sins both in carving and in painting.

I've used two methods of antiquing, both with good results. The first method I've used for years is a mixture of boiled linseed oil and Burnt Umber artist's oil paint. That's about as close as I can come to a recipe for this concoction. I've used it from nearly straight boiled linseed oil to a mixture as black and thick as Cajun coffee. Since no two pieces of wood are alike (especially basswood), it is hard to get a consistent effect. I mix the two in an old blender. Unless you enjoy domestic violence, let me stress that I said an old blender because this stuff is tough to remove. I keep this mixture in an old coffee can with a wide opening so I can completely dip the object. Allow the antiquing to soak in for a few minutes then wipe off all excess mixture with a lint free cloth or paper towel. A small stiff brush is useful in removing any excess from hard to reach areas. The carving should be dry to the touch in a couple of hours and ready for mounting or any gluing that may be needed within 12 to 24 hours.

CAUTION! This mixture is highly flammable and prone to spontaneous combustion. Dispose of all soiled rags and leftovers properly. I got away with being careless with the soiled rags for about 6 years until one night I was awakened by the smoke detector. This potentially disastrous situation left me with only a scorched counter top, but I did become a believer. Keep this mixture sealed in an airtight container and dispose of all soiled rags or paper towels properly.

The second type of finish is a wax finish that I learned from Fort Worth woodcarver, Claude W. Bolton. Its advantages are: it's less messy, it's easy to store, it's less likely to be combustible, and the finish is easily restored by buffing. Many of my carving friends who travel extensively will find this method much easier to transport.

Ingredients:

    Minwax Paste Wax (clear)
    Boiled Linseed Oil
    Turpenoid (odorless turpentine)

Mix all three ingredients in equal parts in a double boiler or old crock pot. The paste wax must be melted to get a complete blend. Allow the new compound to cool and then apply evenly to the carving with an old toothbrush. Be sure to remove any excess wax. Buff with a clean brush. The finish can be renewed by buffing again or applying another coat of wax.

It is possible to create a little darker finish by adding a small amount of artist's oil Burnt Umber to the ingredients. Add just a little at a time and test on a scrap piece of wood until the desired effect is achieved.

This mixture is also good to use on unpainted (natural finish) carvings. If you find that the end grain soaks up too much stain, try lightly sealing the wood with an equal mixture of clear sanding sealer and denatured alcohol.

Since both of these methods produce good results and have their own advantages and disadvantages, and since each piece of wood accepts stain a little differently, some experimentation is recommended until you get the look that suits your needs.

Natural/Clear Finish

There are few things more beautiful and appealing than a natural wood finish. Even boring basswood can be beautiful if properly finished. If you have chosen a beautifully grained wood like catalpa or butternut, then, by all means, don't cover it with paint. I have used two methods successfully. The first is really simple. Deft Natural Finish Spray can be sprayed lightly to seal and protect the wood. Be careful not to spray too heavy since it may leave a shiny, artificial effect.

The second method to use is an equal mixture of clear sanding sealer and denatured alcohol. The piece can be dipped or brushed in the mixture. When dry, this method will leave basswood with a pleasing light golden color that will show off your good clean knife and chisel cuts.

If these two methods still need something more, Clear Minwax or the wax antiquing recipe that you'll find in the antiquing section can be applied to give you a darker finish.

Staining

While staining a caricature carving can have dramatic results, most carvers are not pleased with their efforts because of uneven distribution of the stain. Exposed end-grain of basswood absorbs much more of the stain than does the flat grain, sometimes giving the finished piece a disappointing blotched appearance. The best way to remedy this problem is to lightly seal the wood to control the absorption rate. Use a compatible sealer as recommended for your chosen stain or lightly spray with Deft to seal the wood.

This is a listing of the paints used to finish the projects in this book. These numbers correspond to Ceramcoat by Delta, Artist's Acrylic Paints. This is by no means my complete list of paints since I am not very adept at mixing colors. They all end up an ugly shade of brownish black. You could get by with fewer colors if you can mix colors.

2015	Purple
2021	Dark Chocolate
2023	Brown Iron Oxide
2027	Bright Yellow
2025	Burnt Umber
2029	Caucasian Flesh
2030	Burnt Sienna
2042	Pumpkin
2051	Copen Blue
2068	Christmas Green
2075	Maroon
2078	Straw
2089	Navy Blue
2092	Old Parchment
2104	Fjord Blue
2106	Bonnie Blue
2108	Palomino
2126	Medium Flesh
2127	Dark Flesh
2133	Cape Cod
2431	Mudstone
2503	Bright Red
2505	White
2506	Black
6002	Kim Gold
6003	Silver 7004 Waterbase Varnish

CHAPTER 6
Caricature Ideas, Tips and Not So Secret Secrets

After a few years of caricature carving a lot of my carving started to look very similar. I was running out of new ideas. So I did what any good carver does, I started stealing ideas. Well not exactly, but every time I saw a good idea I would write it down as something to try later. I refer to the list often to stimulate new ideas especially when I want something unique. This list is in no particular order, and not complete by any means. I am constantly adding to it. Any new ideas that you can share with me will be gratefully added to the list.

Caricature Ideas

CLOTHING:

General
- Wrinkled
- Faded/New
- Dirty/Stained
- Frayed/Ragged Hems
- Holes/Tears/Patched
- Patched
- Buttons missing
- Unbutton/Unzipped
- Rolled up Sleeves/Pants
- Too long
- Too loose/baggy
- Too tight/stretched at buttons
- Belts too long

Shirts/Jackets/Coats/Vest
- Tails out, half in/out
- T-shirt logos
- Long johns
- Quilted/down-filled
- Fringe
- Western Yoke
- Plaid/Stripes
- Rolled up sleeves

- Mismatched buttons
- Rainslicker/duster
- 3-piece suits

Accessories
- Ties -- regular, bow, bolo (untied, crooked, uneven)
- Glasses/monocle
- Gloves
- Hankies/Bandana
- Dew Rags
- Headband
- Suspenders
- Garter (sleeves)
- Apron/Bib
- Watch and chain
- Spurs
- Bandana wrapped around and over hat
- Flower in lapel
- Belt too long
- Name on belts
- Buckles too large

Pants/Jeans
- Faded/New
- Tucked into boots
- Too long, drag round in back
- Rolled up
- Half in/out of boots
- Too short (high water)
- Wrinkles behind knees
- Faded at knees and seat
- Snuffcan ring on back pocket
- Chaps (batwing, chinks, woolies)
- Levi patch/Wrangler brand
- Overalls
- Baggy butt

Shoes/Boots/Socks
- One on/one off
- Holes in shoe or boot (side, toe, bottom)
- Mismatched socks

Socks falling down
Toes sticking out
Shoes on wrong feet
Worn on sides from stirrups

Hats/Caps
Bent/floppy brims
Holes with/without hair sticking out
Bullet holes
Bites taken out
Feathers
Gimme caps with logos
Hair sticking out of vent
Visors
See Claude Bolton's book
Heads, Hats and Hair

Props/Things to carry
Hats/caps
Tobacco -- cigar, cigarettes, pipes
(snuff, chewing, roll your own,
spittoon, Bull Durham bags, butts
on floor, burn ends with wood-
burner)
Liquor - - bottles, cans, mug, glass
Cane/walking stick, crutch
Tools -- ropes, branding iron, cattle
prod, knives, post-hole digger
Guns
Toothpick, matches, weeds in mouth
Sports equipment

PHYSICAL FEATURES:

Facial
Black eyes
Wide-eyed
Squinting
Winking
Eyes looking anywhere but straight
Hair in eye/eyes
Smiles, frowns, scowl, sneer
Overbite (bucktooth)
Underbite (bulldog look)
Gritted/grinding teeth
Toothless/sunken cheeks
Missing teeth
Gold tooth
Tongue sticking out

Double chin/wattles
Large or unusual nose
Broken noses

Hands/Arms
Larger than reality
Hand in pockets (front/back)
Thumbs in belt/pockets
Gesturing
Clinched fists
Scratching/picking nose
Arms folded/crossed (front or back)
Hands grasping lapels
Arm in sling/bandaged

Feet/Legs
Larger than reality
Staggered feet
Pigeon-toed
East-West feet
Standing -- weight on one leg
Crossed on one leg
Knock-kneed
Bowlegged

Body Positions
Upright
Slouching/slumped
Bent over, hands on knee
Seated (slouching, slumped, asleep,
feet crossed, staggered, propped up)
Squatting
Kneeling
Crawling
Leaning against objects
Lying down, face up or down
Carrying objects
Walking
Running

Fat Bodies
Pear-shaped
Sway-backed
Knock-Kneed
East-west feet
Pot/beer belly
Small or big butts
Double chins

Skinny Bodies

   Slouching (poor posture)
   Spoon-chested
   Bowlegged
   Pidgeon-toed
   Pot/beer belly

Tips and Not-So-Secret Secrets

V-tools cut more than a v-trough in the wood. It will cut right, left, and center. Learn to use either side to create dramatic shadow effect. This is especially important if you use natural finishes.

Feet patterns -- If you have trouble carving matching feet, make a small pattern of either foot then turn the pattern over and you will have a pattern for the opposite foot.

Texture -- For beard stubble, fabric texture, animal fur, wool, or woolen long johns, I use a small electric engraver. This tool also works well to texture bases for your carvings. Tips can be sharpened or blunted for different textures.

Beards -- I make beard stubble and five o'clock shadow a little differently than most other carvers. I never could get the hang of the v-tool and dry brush method that most carvers use. I use a sharpened awl or the electric engraver to texture the beard. If using the water thinned flesh-tone swells the wood and closes the holes, apply the beard texture after painting. Apply a very thin wash of black which sinks into the holes leaving a stubble effect.

Buttons are easily made with a small half round gouge. Make opposite cuts with the end of the gouge to form the round button. Be sure that each half of the button angles away from the center or the button will pop out. Relieve a small amount of wood from the top and bottom to make the bottom stand out. A sharpened awl or nail can be used to make thread holes but be careful not to split the button.

For carving thin, carved pieces such as a rope, a horses rein, or harness, I use the material from a Christmas wreath. I'm not sure exactly what it is, maybe a grapevine, but it is wood. It can be purchased at most craft stores. When soaked in soapy water or Windex it is easily bent or twisted to the desired shape. Allow it to dry in that configuration and it will remain. You can now carve it to the thickness you want.

Snow -- I recently discovered a commercial product at the craft store called Snow-Tex Textural Medium that produces a good snow effect. It's much better than white painted basswood because it adds texture.

Eye highlights -- A small speck of white on the eye pupil adds life to the eye. For a shiny, glossy effect on the eyeball, try clear fingernail polish or Ceramcoat by Delta Waterbase Varnish #7004.

To make the spines on cactus cut bristles from an old natural bristle paint brush. Use an awl or sharpened nail to make a hole to receive the spine. Use tweezers and dip the end of the bristle in glue and insert it into the cactus. Trim it to the right length when dry.

A couple of hairs on a big wart are also easily created by using the above technique.

Keep a small mirror in your tool box. Use it to check facial expressions. We often incorrectly assume that the face does a certain thing. Make faces in the mirror to check for correct structure. Hint: Don't do this in the presence of others.

Use a woodburner to burn the ends of cigarettes and cigars for a more realistic touch.

Knife blade shape -- I prefer a large, stiff blade with no flex at all. I like the cutting edge to be perfectly straight. I feel that the straight edge and no flex eliminates some of the "variables" and gives me greater control. The blade should taper both in thickness and width to a fine point. The flat bevel runs from the cutting edge all the way up to the top edge. Fine tune the top edge of the blade by rounding it so the blade "rolls" out of the wood without "chattering". This style of knife allows me to move lots of wood yet carve fine detail.

Bases and Mounting

I usually mount all of my carvings on a base. The main reason is to protect them from being knocked over and broken, but it also provides a space for a title or catchy humorous saying. Don't get too elaborate with the base. Remember that the base should not attract attention from the carving itself but rather protect and enhance the presentation of the carving.

I use a small dowel to secure the carving to the base and most of the time use ordinary wood glue, unless the carving or base is exceptionally large or heavy.

I prefer to use a base 1 1/4" to 2" in thickness. A quarter round router bit makes a simple neat edge that will allow room for a title, caption, or engraved name plate.

Wood flooring is my personal favorite for my western style carvings. Old oak strip flooring is made with a woodburning tool or v-tool. Be sure to include knot holes, splits, nails and texture. Varying shades of brown, black, and grey will help add age and character to the flooring.

A base carved to look like stone, rock, or brick also makes an attractive presentation.

Irregularly shaped bases are visually more interesting than rounds, squares, and rectangles especially if you can artistically balance the shape of the base and carving.

CHAPTER 7
Read More About It

I have all of the following books in my personal library, and I heartily recommend them to anyone who is serious about improving as a caricature woodcarver. While not all of these are carving books they are all excellent sources for those interested in human anatomy and the art of caricature.

Another excellent source of ideas and caricature patterns is coloring books. Toys R Us and Children's Palace in my area have good selections of coloring books and comic books.

BOLTON, Claude W.
Carving Cowboy Faces
Carving Cowboys
Carving Heads, Hats, and Hair

BRAGONIER, Reginald
What's What, a Visual Glossary of the Physical World

This book is an invaluable source of information about anything and everything you might ever want to carve.

BRIDGMAN, George B.
The Book of a Hundred Hands
Heads, Features and Faces
Bridgman's Life Drawing

ENLOW, Harold L.
Carving Western Figures
How to Carve Hobos
Learn to Carve Faces and Expressions

Enlow has also written other good carving books all of which have excellent sharpening instructions.

GAUTIER, Dick
The Art of Caricature
The Creative Cartoonist

HAMM, Jack
Cartooning the Head and Figure
Drawing the Head and Figure

HIGGINBOTHAM, Bill
Carving Country Characters
Humnorous Country Characters
Folk Characters

HOGARTH, Burne
Drawing Dynamic Hands
Dynamic Figure Drawing
Dynamic Anatomy
Drawing the Human Head

REDMAN, Lenn
How to Draw Caricatures

CHAPTER 8
Projects 1 - 15

Project 1 - Confused Cowboy

Project 2 - Cowboy P.H.D., the Post Hole Digger

Project 3 - Rummy Belcher, Town Drunk

Project 4 - Ricky Wreck, the Rank Bull Rider

Project 5 - The Cowboy Cowboy Carver

Project 6 - Cowtown Santa, the Reluctant Santa Claus

Project 7 - Doc Croakum, Country Doctor

Project 8 - Digger Dirge, the Undertaker

Project 9 - "Broncitis", Bronco Busted Cowboy

Project 10 - Shady Schyster, Lawyer of Cheatum, Pettifogger, Crook, and Schyster

Project 11 - Brother Paul, the Circuit Riding Preacher

Project 12 - Sage Soliloquy, Town Philosopher

Project 13 - Bad Dude Bandit

Project 14 - The Tailgater

Project 15 - Slug Hazard, Rodeo Clown

Confused Cowboy

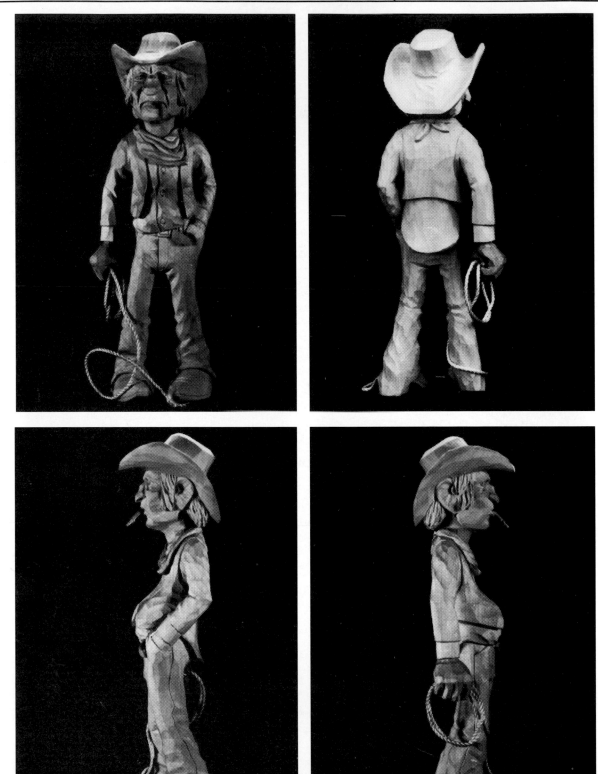

PROJECT 1
Confused Cowboy

This original carving is in the collection of Harold Enlow, Dogpatch, Arkansas.

Cowboyn' is hard, exhaustive work, from before dawn till can't. Surviving on strong coffee, beans, and beef jerky, this cowboy's weary body with slumping posture, drooped shoulders, and sagging expression, shows just how hard his life really is. This dog-tired old cowboy with an empty rope seems to be saying, "I'm so tired, I don't know if I found a rope or lost a horse."

Carving this "good ole boy" is pretty much standard work for anyone who has ever carved a cowboy. There are a few subtleties though, that bear mentioning. Notice that the legs arc staggered and that he stands a little pigeon-toed. There is also one toe up and one down. In profile, he is spoon-chested, pot-bellied, and round-shouldered. This stance gives him a more relaxed, interesting posture. Many woodcarvings look too stiff and static. Avoid equal balance, both arms and feet in the same positions.

Wrinkles add action, catch and reflect light, and generally make the carving more interesting. Add wrinkles inside the elbows, behind the knees, and above the instep. Don't make the wrinkles uniform by using a v-tool. I use my knife to make wedge cuts in an irregular pattern. Carving cleanly doesn't mean that the carving has to be smooth and boring.

The extra-length belt is an added piece on this one. The hair is textured with a small veiner (deep u-gouge). The grasping/clenched right hand is carved separately and inserted. I used to think that adding pieces was somehow cheating until I learned that this method has been used by the great master carvers for centuries.

The face on this fellow really needs to sag. I used the old, bagged eye to emphasize this look. The mouth is down-turned. Even his roll-your-own cigarette is drooping. Five o'clock shadowing on the face completes the look. (See Chapter 6)

Paint & Finish

Black	2506	Hair, pants, boots, belt
Silver	6003	Buckle
Mudstone	2431	Hat
Christmas Green	2068	Bandana
Fjord Blue	2104	Shirt

The following colors are basic for flesh tones and eye colors for all of the carvings to follow and will not be repeated for each project. (See Chapter 5)

Medium Flesh	2126	Base flesh tone
Caucasian Flesh	2029	Highlights, nose, cheeks, lips
Cape Cod	2133	Iris of the eyes

Finish with Boiled Linseed Oil and burnt umber antiquing solution. (See Chapter 5)

Cowboy P.H.D. (Post Hole Digger)

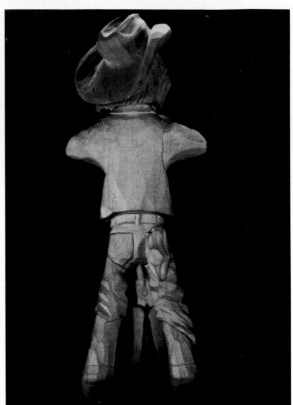

PROJECT 2
Cowboy P.H.D. (Post Hole Digger)

This original carving is in the collection of Alan and Evelyn MacKay, Welling, Alberta, Canada.

Not all cowboy work is done from astride a horse. The days of the open range are long gone. One of the worst jobs for the ranch hand cowboy was fence building, particularly digging the postholes. The ground was nearly always dry and hard, or, as we have many places here in Texas, solid rock a few inches under the surface. It is tough, blister-busting, back-breaking toil in the hot sun. Many a cowboy has received his education (P.H.D.) from the University of Hard Knocks. Digging post holes for long, lonely hours helped develop this cowboy's philosophy of life. Most everyone has spent at least a little time (it just seemed like an eternity) with one of these tools and can relate to this poor cowboy's misery.

The P.H.D. cowboy's posture has the knees locked, hips thrust forward and back arched to counter balance the weight of the post hole diggers. His rolled up sleeves and pants stuffed in his boots show he is seriously attacking this job. His ragged, unkept hair betrays the fact that he hasn't been to town for a store-bought haircut in a long time.

The gloved hands and arms are carved separately on this figure too. It's easier to fit the post hole diggers to the hands using this method. They are basic grasping/clenched hand types.

The face is weathered and worn. The mustache is long enough to cover the lips. The eyes are drooping and bagged. The head is carved separately and turned as if he is day dreaming about more pleasant times or Saturday nights in town.

Be sure to add a dirty sweat stain around the crown of the hat. This hat brim is also rolled more than on other projects in this book.

Paint & Finish

Mudstone	2431	Hat, gloves
Brown Iron Oxide	2023	Boots, vest, post hole diggers
Burnt Sierra	2030	Boot uppers, belt
Black	2506	Hair, post hole diggers
Pumpkin	2042	Shirt
Parchment	2092	Longjohns
Silver	6003	Buckle, post hole diggers
Bright Red	2503	Bandana

Flesh and eyes as in Project #1

Finish with Boiled Linseed Oil and Burnt umber antiquing solution.

PROJECT 5
The Cowboy Cowboy Carver

This original carving is in the collection of Richard Spinney, Beaumont, Texas.

The Cowboy Cowboy Carver is probably a misnomer since, by strict definition, he is actually a whittler. Whatever you call him, he is having fun. In years past, almost every man and young boy carried a pocket knife, and most were skillful whittlers. By comparison, today's generation has little time or patience to enjoy the pleasure of a sharp knife slicing through wood. Most cowboys today still carry a pocket knife as a utility tool for such varied uses as a hoof pick, wire cutter, toothpick, can opener, castration tool, or splinter remover. In what little spare time a working cowboy might have, he may find whittling is nothing more than idly making chips by sharpening the nearest available stick. His choice of subjects here is what he knows best, a cowboy.

Carving a seated figure really isn't very difficult except that there is more wood to carve by hand since the bandsaw cannot remove as much as on a stand-up figure. Arms and legs that run cross-grain require sharp tools and are easily broken if too much pressure is applied. I confess to sometimes using a power tool with a Kutzall bit to remove wood more quickly and with less pressure between the arms and legs.

Notice that the legs and arms are staggered again. One knee is out more with the foot slightly angled. My southpaw carving friend, Dave Dunham, was quick to note that this carver is a lefty. This was not intentional on my part but can be easily adjusted to the "right" way if you so desire. The elbow holding the piece should be closer to the body while the other elbow is farther away from the body. The knife hand is just a clenched fist. The other hand can be carved with the whittled piece in it or inserted into the hand later. The fingers cradle the piece with the thumb holding it in place. I carved the hands separately on this one since it's easier to clean up the midsection area without them in the way.

The small cowboy was carved from a 1/2" x 1/2" x 5" piece and cut off when complete. Keeping my big fingers out of the way is near impossible unless I carve it on the stick.

I used a chair for this cowboy to sit on but in the past have used a box, tree stump or even a pile of rocks. Anything will work as long as the seating height is correct.

The hat, ears, nose and mustache are all exaggerated on this cowboy. I wanted him to appear to be older, so I used deep set eyes with deep wrinkles and creases around them. The eyes are horizontally modified cartoon eyes that are barely opened.

Paint & Finishing

No paint		Small cowboy
Burnt Sienna	2030	Hat
Palomino	2108	Shirt
Black	2506	Hair, boots
Navy Blue	2809	Jeans
Silver	6003	Knife blade

Flesh tone and the eyes as described in Project #1.
Finish with boiled linseed oil and Burnt Umber antiquing solution.

PROJECT 6
Cowtown Santa

This original carving is in the collection of Jack and Shirley Sugden, Edmonton, Alberta, Canada.

Christmas in the Fort Worth Stockyards is little different than other commercial tourist areas. The stores start early and push it hard. I actually saw a "Santa" that looked like this character down there. He obviously had been taking in, as well as spreading, "Christmas cheer." His ill-fitting Santa suit, combined with traditional western garb, betrayed his true identity. Although his need to present a rough tough image would never allow him to admit to enjoying his role as Santa Claus, most cowboys have a big, tender heart under that crusty exterior.

While there is a lot of detail on the Cowtown Santa, basically, he is just a straight up and down cowboy. The head is carved separately and so are the toys. The baggy Santa suit distorts most of the body outline, but keep in mind that you are carving a skinny cowboy underneath the baggy suit. The pants are stuffed into the boots. I suppose fancy stitching on the boot shaft would be appropriate. Just don't get carried away and make them too gaudy.

The bent arm hand is clutching the toy bag material. The fingers on the top of the hand are carved into the end grain. Use a sharp tool and a slicing action here. The other hand, hanging at his side, is in the same basic position. Both hands are gloved and therefore bulkier.

The pillow used to fatten the cowboy has slipped. The belt is cinched tightly around the pillow. He has a large rodeo belt buckle.

The bag was hollowed out and the toys were added but the bag and toys can be carved as all one piece if you prefer. The bag can be textured in a cross-hatch pattern with a small v-tool or even a power tool to stimulate a burlap bag.

The head and hat are a little different. The Santa cap is fitted over the cowboy hat, and you'll need to plan ahead to leave enough wood. The expression is not happy. A gaunt, worn look with squinting, bagged eyes works well here. The fake Santa beard has fallen down to the chin. His dark hair and beard stubble are exposed.

Paint & Finishing

Bright Red	2503	Santa suit and cap
White	2505	Santa suit trim, pillow
Silver	6003	Buckle
Brown Iron Oxide	2023	Boots, bag
Burnt Sienna	2030	Boots, belt, hat
Mudstone	2431	Pillow
Various colors		Toys
Kim Gold	6002	Buckle

Flesh tones and eyes as described in Project #1.

Finish with Boiled Linseed Oil and Burnt Umber antiquing solution.

Doc Croakum

PROJECT 7
Doc Croakum

This original carving is in the collection of Al and Helga Kapusta, Calgary, Alberta, Canada.

Very few people were respected or loved in the community more than the country doctor. His willingness to make do with whatever, whenever, and wherever made him an invaluable part of western life. Unlike today's physicians, he was not always well equipped, highly educated, or well-paid. He was often paid with whatever his patients could afford. In this caricature, he has received a live chicken in exchange for services rendered. Dressed neatly but not expensively, in his three piece suit, string tie, gold watch and chain, and a small brimmed hat all give evidence of this man's place of prominence in the community. His hair is neatly trimmed and his handlebar mustache hugs the contour of his face. His stance indicates pride in his profession, even when carrying an undignified, acrimonious live chicken under his arm.

The left hand is a clenched/grasping hand around the handle of his little black bag. The right hand is slightly cupped (a relaxed hand variation) with the fingers and thumbs almost parallel to each other.

The face of this little fellow is neat and clean even though he looks a little tired, perhaps having returned from a late night house call. Remember house calls? The focal point of this face is the neatly groomed handle bar mustache. Its graceful curve and drop are matched by the curve and drop of the eyes which are modified versions of the cartoon eye. The drooping upper lid accents the tired, aged look. The upper lip is covered with only the lower lip exposed.

The hat is small and stylish, rather than the large functional type. The hair is gouged, then v-tooled.

The chicken, on this prototype, was an added piece but recently I have been carving the chicken as one piece with the body.

Paint and Finishing

Black	2506	Hat, tie, belt, shoes, bag
White	2505	Shirt, chicken, hair
Pumpkin	2042	Chicken beak
Fjord Blue	2104	3 Piece suit
Kim Gold	6002	Watch chain, buckle
Mudstone	2431	Hair
Bright Red	2503	Chicken comb

The fleshtone and eyes are painted as in the previous projects.

Finish with antiquing solution.

PROJECT 8
Digger Dirge, the Undertaker

This original carving is in the collection of Ronnie and Vaudine Dulin, Lubbock, Texas.

This stereotypical version of an old west mortician appears in this caricature as a slick, unscrupulous figure who willingly undertakes an unavoidable chore that most of us consider unthinkable. The somber black dress doesn't disguise this fellow's love of life and sometimes irreverent attitude. In all fairness, this really is an unjust characterization of this profession. Most of them are upstanding, honest, caring professionals. (My good friend, "Digger Dulin" made me put that in.)

The body and clothing of this carving are very similar to Doc Croakum, except that he is obviously taller and more slender. The top hat adds even more height to his stature. The main differences here are the arm and leg positions. He has more weight on his right leg. The left leg is relaxed and turned outward. This position throws the right hip outward which provides a resting place for the back of the right hand.

The upside down positioning of the right hand confused me for a short time until I finally figured out that by rotating my own right hand to a position right in front of me, I had a ready model. This hand is actually just a relaxed hand turned upside down. The left hand was carved separately and added. He grips the cigar with a modified two finger and thumb grip. The ring and little finger are opened, indicating a carefree, almost arrogant posture.

The top hat is the most dominant part of the separately carved head. I chose a straight forward attitude for its position on the head. Tilting it with its extreme height presents some additional problems I wished to avoid. If you want to tilt it for a more jaunty look, refer to Claude Bolton's book, *Heads, Hats and Hair*. His W. C. Fields bust is a good example of a tilted top hat.

The face sports a very large nose, close-set, narrow eyes, large mustache, and toothy grin. The nose is so large and overhanging that the mustache appears to be coming out of each nostril. This mustache does not conform to the shape of the face as it did with Doc Croakum, but rather it extends straight out. This makes the tips very fragile and difficult to texture. I find the small veiner works better for this texturing than does the v-tool. Follow the curve of the mustache by rolling the veiner over and under the mustache. This will give the effect of the mustache having been twisted or curled.

The regular type eyes are rather deep-set, and the pupils are positioned in the corners for a sneaky appearance. The brow ridge line is left heavy to accent the deep set look.

Paint & Finish

Black (various shades)	2506	3-Piece suit, tie, hat, shoes
White	2505	Shirt
Burnt Umber	2025	Hair, cigar
Kim Gold	6002	Watch chain, buckle

Flesh tones and eyes as in previous projects.

Finish with antiquing solution.

"Bronc-itis"

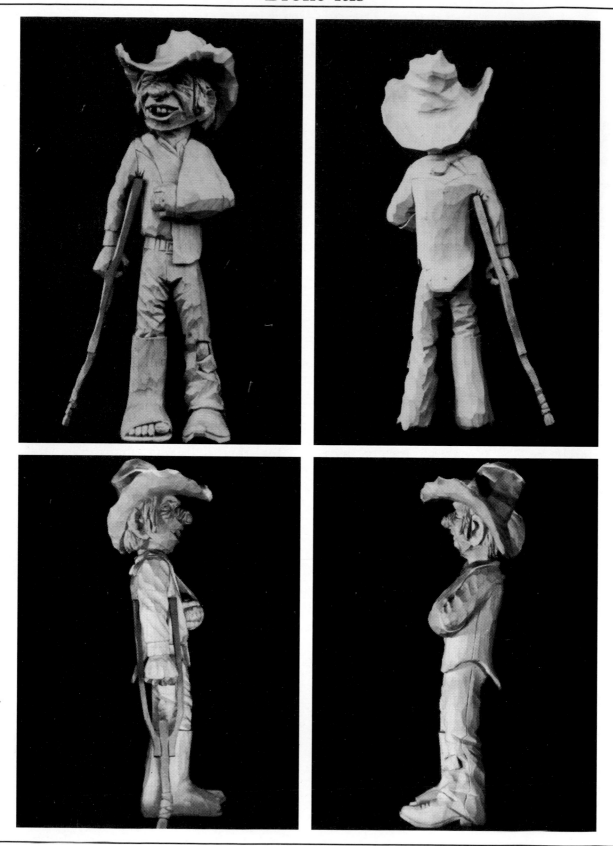

PROJECT 9
"Bronc-itis"

This original carving is in the collection of David M. Dunham, Cleburne, Texas.

A cowboy is just a hired hand on horseback. The cowboy and his horse share a special love-hate relationship. It was often said, "Approach a horse the same way a porcupine makes love: slow and careful." To transform a wild, ornery, bronco into a trustworthy working partner is no easy task. This bronco-busted cowpoke illustrates just how physically demanding it is to break horses. One leg in a cast, an arm in a sling, a broken nose, black eye, torn and soiled clothing, a rumpled hat, and even a bandaged crutch all point to the diagnosis of "Bronc-itis".

From the front view, this cowboy looks fairly balanced, but when viewed from behind you'll notice that the crutch supported shoulder is higher and that the body leans backward slightly in an unsteady position.

The crutch needs to be carved fairly early in this project because its fit to the hand and under the arm is critical. The crutch is purposely carved crooked and bandaged to match this poor cowboy's condition. The hand pictured here was carved as one piece with the body. I have also carved this piece with hand separate and inserted it into the sleeve. Whichever way you carve, the crutch bows are carved to fit snugly around the hand. The handpiece is removed and glued into the clenched fist later, after the final fit is achieved. The sling arm elbow must be in front of the chest, the lower arm parallel to it. The finger tips extend past the midline of the chest. The shirt tail is out three-fourths of the way.

The legs and feet are carved next. The toes on the cast foot should not be all in the same plane. (Example: small toes down, big toe up.) The cast has very little shape. You might want to substitute a bandaged foot for the cast. The tear at the knee is not just a hole. Notice that the flap is hanging down to expose the knee. Other tears in the clothing or patches might be appropriate, too.

This cowboy's face is a little more challenging to carve. Partly because of the detail and partly because the hat is pulled down on the head. The nose has no detail since it's covered by the bandage. His right eye is swollen shut and blackened. This is easy to carve since its just the eye mound (see Chapter 2, Step 4) with the eye slit carved across it. Wrinkles are added for accent. The open eye is a regular eye with upper eye lid arched. The pupil is positioned at the bottom of the eye since he is smiling. The big toothy grin is obviously missing one tooth. Be sure to undercut and backcut the teeth to create a shadow effect. Add beard stubble also. The hat is very wrinkled and beat up and the hair is shaggy and separated at the ends as if dirty or sweaty.

Paint & Finishing

Black	2506	Hat
Christmas Green	2068	Shirt
Navy Blue	2089	Jeans
Dark Chocolate	2021	Boot, belt
White	2505	Sling, cast, bandages on nose and fingers
Natural		Crutch

Flesh tones and eyes as in previous projects.

Finish with antiquing solution.

Shady Schyster - Lawyer of Cheatum, Crook, Pittifogger and Schyster

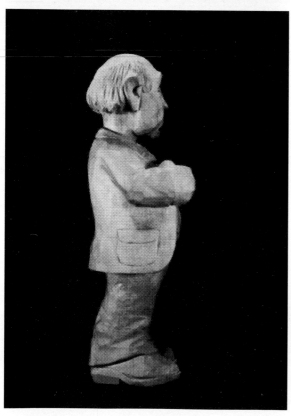 

PROJECT 10
Shady Schyster
Lawyer of Cheatum, Crook, Pettifogger and Schyster

This original carving is in the collection of Ivan and Trudy Rossiter, Wichita, Kansas.

In recent years lawyers have really taken a lot of abuse. Some of it deserved, some not. (Who doesn't know at least one good lawyer joke.) Maybe it's because it has become so common to sue or be sued in today's society that we've all had dealings with members of the bar, usually in unpleasant situations. Don't let this short, round, balding figure fool you. This old country counselor may appear to be an easy adversary when in reality he is as wise as a tree full of owls and tough enough to have a reserved seat in hell. (Which is where many think lawyers belong anyway.) His proud stance is typical as he pleads his case before the bar.

The Shady Schyster figure can also be carved as a pompous politician or a prosperous banker. The clothing is basically the same as the doctor, undertaker, and preacher, so we won't spend time describing it again.

Most caricature cowboy figures are tall and lanky. By contrast, this figure is squatty and rather full-bodied. Several observations about the anatomy of a portly figure should be noted before we begin carving. The porcine body must stand sway-backed in order to counter balance the weight of the heavy potbelly out in front. The more rotund figure also tends to stand equally on both feet to evenly distribute his corpulence. The short, stocky legs are straight, with knees locked to control the mass. The heavyset person's toes generally turn outward, giving an east-west appearance to the feet. The tilt of the head is forward and down accenting the fleshy double chin and jowly cheeks. If the arms were at his side, they would be behind the mid-line of the body. Caricature the chubby face by making the lower part of the face wider than the upper (narrow at the temples and wide at the cheeks). Did you notice how I described all that without calling him fat? Mama would be proud of me.

Both hands here are really just modified clenched fists. The last set of knuckles on the lapel are hidden and require the coat to be pulled away from the body slightly. The gesturing hand was carved separately and inserted. It is nothing more than the clenched fist with one finger extended.

The face shape is blocked-in very early. Remember, narrower at the temples, wider at the cheeks and jowls. The mouth is open with teeth and tongue exposed. The eyes are modified regular eyes with the lower lid nearly straight. The upper lid is arched and the pupils rolled upward as if appealing to a higher power. The brow ridge is heavy and the eyebrows are wild and bushy -- which seems to be a requirement for politicians or for anyone holding public office in most southern states.

The balding head accents the narrowness of the upper head and is in contrast to the wider, lower part. The hair is v-tooled and is longer at its ends.

Paint & Finishing

Mudstone	2431	3-piece suit
White	2505	Shirt
Black	2506	Shoes, belt, tie
Burnt Sienna	2030	Hair
Kim Gold	6002	Watch chain

Flesh tones and eyes as described in Project #1.

Finish with Boiled Linseed Oil and Burnt Umber antiquing solution.

PROJECT 11
Brother Paul, the Circuit Riding Preacher

This original carving is in the collection of Hurston and Elsie Prescott, Winnsboro, Texas.

The circuit riding preacher did not have a regular pulpit from which to sermonize. Often, his podium was on horseback or in a shady grove of trees -- anywhere a few faithful could be gathered. His sermons could be Bible pounding, hell-fire-and-brimstone orations or simple, homespun country parables. The Bible and the parson's hat are both essential tools of the trade -- the first for spiritual support and second for financial support.

This prototype parson turned out rather solemn looking, almost as if preaching a funeral. His posture and the angle of the neck and head would also suggest some sadness or heavy burden. If you prefer a more upbeat clergyman, then just change the angle of the head, neck and expression.

The clothing of the circuit riding preacher is a little different. The long black coat is slightly more than mid-thigh in length. It was meant to serve the dual purpose of a dress coat and as protection on horseback, like today's duster. The pants are stuffed into high top, smooth shaft uppers. The double breasted vest may be a bit ostentatious for a minister, but perhaps he is just a forerunner of today's more flamboyant TV evangelists. The black string tie is a little broader than in earlier projects. The hat brim has very little curve.

The right and left hands are almost identical. They are modified relaxed hands.

The thumb is rotated to the midline of the hand and fingers to grip the Bible and hat.

The head is carved separately here, but it certainly would be no problem to carve as one piece. The full head of hair is his crowning glory and a bit stereotypical of some preachers, country and western singers, and flim flam men. The long sideburns and slightly receding hairline can be exaggerated. The hair is given a flowing look by using a gouge, rather than a v-tool to texture it. The eyes are the old, bagged eye type. The upper bag is accented with the lower bag less obvious. Crow's feet wrinkles at the corners of the eyes show more time spent out in the sun, traveling and preaching outdoors.

The mouth and nose are extra wide. The downturned mouth extends nearly to the outside corners of the eye.

The Bible and hat were added. The Bible is old and worn and therefore limber. Don't carve it too straight and stiff. The hat shouldn't have much curve to the brim.

Paint & Finishing

Black (various shades)	2506	Boots, hat, tie and Bible
White	2505	Shirt, Bible
Burnt Sienna	2030	Hair
Silver	6003	Buckle

Flesh tones and eyes as described in Project #1.

Finish with Boiled Linseed Oil and Burnt Umber antiquing solution.

PROJECT 12
Sage Soliloquy, Town Philosopher

This original carving is in the collection of Frank Eldred, Albuquerque, New Mexico.

Sage Soliloquy is always ready to give advice on any subject at any time. His knowledge of the subject does not limit his verbose rambling as he attempts to convert all within earshot to his way of thinking. Although he may look different today, there's always one of these guys in every group. You'll probably recognize one at your work, church, or even in your carving club. Incredible as it may seem, many have accused me of using some of my fellow Texans as a model for this project.

This street-corner orator is at home with his role in the community, and with his slanted philosophy of life. His demeanor is reflected in his relaxed, easygoing posture. His hand and arm are resting across his bent leg. All of his weight is supported on the straight leg, which throws his hip out slightly. The knee on the bent leg is angled outward also. Other than those few observations, he's pretty much a standard cowboy from a carver's point of view.

I suggest that you keep the bandsawed piece from under his foot for support and dowel the straight leg to a base otherwise this figure will not stand and that will make it harder to keep your perspective as the carving progresses.

The gesturing hand is a pointing hand (see Chapter 4 or Shady Schyster, Project 10). It is turned almost as if he were poking his finger into the other guy's chest to drive home his point.

The head is carved separately. The hair is a little shaggy and has been v-tooled for texture. Its a little hard to see because of his gesturing hand, but there is a large wad of chewing tobacco that distorts the shape of the face. The corner of the mouth is almost in alignment with the outside corner of the eye on chew side of the face. This side is also more closed (tight-lipped to prevent leakage) as if he is speaking out of the other side. The nose is very broad (center to center of the eyes). The eyes are rolled upward, brows arched with pupils placed high. These eyes are the modified cartoon eyes or widened regular eyes. The ears are large and flopped out at the top edge.

The wrinkling on the bent leg is interesting and will really catch and reflect light if executed properly. I use a thin blade, pointed in a rolling action, to get the effect of the material being pulled toward the knee area. A gouge makes the wrinkles too consistent.

I recommend that this figure be dowelled onto a base to prevent breakage.

Paint & Finishing

Palomino	2108	Shirt
Fjord Blue	2104	Bandana
Navy Blue	2089	Jeans
Mudstone	2431	Hat
Dark Chocolate	2021	Boot and belt
Silver	6003	Buckle

Flesh tones and eyes as in previous project.

Finish with antiquing solution.

Bad Dude Bandit

PROJECT 13
Bad Dude Bandit

This original carving is in the collection of Claude and Marcia Lee Bolton, Fort Worth, Texas.

We will always have this element of society regardless of the times in which we live. There will always be those who would rather steal than work, rather do harm than good, or are just downright mean and ornery. This desperado is probably all of the above. His double six-shooters testify to the fact that he is armed and dangerous. The bandana and duster both help to conceal this highwayman's identity from law abiding citizens. This "Bad Dude" is as full of venom as a rattlesnake in August.

The Bad Dude Bandit body can be carved fairly easily. The duster conceals most of the body shape except the small area exposed in the front. The extra large bandana has just slipped down from the outlaw's face. He also has an oversized hat that is pulled down low on the head. He stands equally balanced on both feet ready for action.

The hands and pistols are carved together. They are better carved separate from the body because of the grain and the amount of wood that will be wasted otherwise. This type hand is basically a pointing hand shape. The index just being bent on the last two joints. The pistols are exaggerated in size. Actually if you've ever had a pistol pointed at you in earnest, they probably look about right.

After roughing out the head, I used a Foredom and Kutz-all bit to hollow out the neck area. This way the head and bandana area can be jointly developed. I wanted the entire chin and most of the mouth covered as if the bandana had just slipped enough to reveal part of his face.

With more than half of the face covered, you'll have to do a good job with the exposed area (mainly the eyes) to sell the mean, dangerous look of this badman.

I chose to have narrow slits with the eyes turned to the side for a sneaky look. Raise the eyebrow on that side also. These eyes are regular eyes that have been narrowed for effect.

The nose is broad, flat, and wrinkled across the bridge. There are also bags and creases under the eyes to give a tough, weathered look.

I chose to have him talking out of the side of his mouth. Notice that the mouth is slanted up on that side to reveal some more expression from behind the bandana. The left side photo has the head elevated a little to expose the face more for a better view for the camera.

The hair is long enough to cover the ears and has been gouged, then v-tooled.

Paint & Finishing

Black	2506	Hat, vest, pants, belt, boots, hair, holster
Bright Red	2503	Bandana
Mudstone	2431	Duster
Fjord Blue	2104	Pistols

Flestone and eyes are painted as in previous projects.

Finish with antiquing solution.

The Tailgater

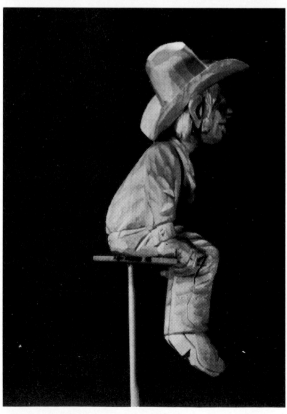

PROJECT 14
The Tailgater

This original carving is in the collection of John and Hazel Chaney, Wichita, Kansas.

No doubt the original tailgate party was held on the back of a chuckwagon with hardtack, beans, and hot coffee as the usual fare. Today's modern cowboy has little need for a chuckwagon because the pickup tailgate has taken its place as a dining table, workbench, operating table, or just a convenient place to sit or rest after the chores are done. The tailgate may also provide a place for impromptu social gatherings to discuss such important topics as the weather or cattle prices.

In this project "The Tailgater" is taking a well-deserved break from ranch chores. On the cover you will note a neat way of mounting and displaying this project. The inspiration for this project came as Dave Stetson and I traveled through ranching country in Wyoming. Most ranches were busy putting up hay for the long winter months ahead. We commented how many were now using the large round bales which are all handled by machines. We both recalled having "hauled hay" enough to know that wasn't what we wanted for the rest of our lives, yet it's a common chore for the cowboy.

The tailgater's posture is tired and relaxed. The shoulders and back should be rounded. Many carved, seated figures look too stiff, too upright. Make this one relaxed. His feet even dangle freely. The bandana also hangs straight down away from the chest. The arms are only slightly bent, not really supporting the body.

The hands are not gripping the tailgate tightly. I chose to take the easy way out and cover the thumbs with the outside of the thighs. A small piece of wood the size and thickness of the tailgate will help in fitting and carving the hands to the proper size at this point. Just carve the hand planes as you have in the past projects.

The neck placement is at an angle so that hair and back brim are resting on the shoulders. The hat is tilted back to expose more of the face. Leave enough wood for the hair on the forehead. Carving the right eye will be easier if the hair is split, placed above the eyebrow, or completely covering the eye. Carving the eye under the hair as I've done is not the way I'd do it again. The eyes are the regular type eye.

Lots of shaggy hair and big floppy ears are prominent features. The hair should be laid out in clumps as if dirty and sweaty.

The most dominant feature, though, is the mouth which extends to the outside corner of each eye. Be sure that the mouth follows the oral curve back into the corners of the mouth (see the left side profile). Exaggerate the size of the teeth also. Notice that even with this big smile, that on the upper level there are only four complete upper teeth visible. Most carvers try to put in a full set of dentures and it looks too busy. Keep it simple and uncluttered. One other thing to watch for here is what I call the "Happy Face Syndrome". Smiles that have both corners of the upper lip curling upward are incorrect. The upper lip stretches tightly across the upper teeth in a straight line and pushes back into the cheeks. The lower lip is the one that really shows the curvature of the smile. Also note that the mandible (lower jaw) swings down and back for the bigger smile or open mouth.

This cowboy can be mounted on a variety of things. A pickup tailgate, tailgate of a covered wagon, a fence rail, table or bench are all potential mounts.

Paint & Finishing

Burnt Sienna	2030	Hat
Parchment	2092	Shirt
Fjord Blue	2104	Bandana
Copen Blue	2051	Jeans
Dark Chocolate	2021	Boots, belt
Burnt Umber	2025	Hair

Fleshtone and eyes as in previous projects.

Finish with antiquing solution.

PROJECT 15
Slug Hazard, Rodeo Clown

This original carving is in the collection of Dave Stetson, Phoenix, Arizona.

The rodeo clown is more than just an entertainer. His real job is to protect other rodeo performers from danger, especially the bullriders. Many rodeo clowns did not begin their rodeo career as clowns but were participants in other rodeo events. Slug Hazard, the rodeo clown, was once a bullrider, but as suggested by his name he is a step or two too slow to be in the rodeo arena. This limitation puts him on the edge of disaster most of the time. The audience thinks it's all part of the act -- which keeps him in demand. He refuses to retire until "bullied" into it.

This high-stepping buffoon has an exaggerated body-lean to show speed and movement. Note that you can almost draw a straight line from the ankle up to the fist. Even the angle of the neck is in the same plane. The hair, bandana, shoe laces and shorts are all trailing in the breeze in another plane. All of these contribute to the illusion of speed. It should also be noted that the faster a person moves, the greater the tendency to single track, which means the legs, feet, arms and hairdo will all move toward the center line of the body. The arms and legs also move in opposite directions on each side to counterbalance each other.

Obviously, this carving will not stand by itself so it will have to be doweled through a fairly thin part of the foot. Be careful not to go all the way through.

The hands were carved separately. Both are clenched fists and will look better if rotated just a little toward the midline. The hands are gloved so it's not necessary to put much detail into them.

The face is distorted by fright. The eyes are the wide-open cartoon type. The more they bulge, the better. The mouth is similar to the Bad Dude Bandit mouth, except both sides are distorted. Create depth and shadow at the corners for the impression that muscles at the sides of the mouth and neck are straining. The wig is textured with a small gouge. Be sure to allow for the trailing effect on the hair. The nose is wrinkled and the brow is furrowed. The hat brim is blown up in the front.

Clown costumes vary a great deal, so nearly anyway you dress yours is acceptable. Just be sure that it is bright, oversized or outlandish. The make-up on a clown is different on each one and is like their own signature, so feel free to design your own make-up pattern.

Paint & Finishing

Maroon	2075	Hat
Fjord Blue	2104	Shorts
Purple	2015	Shirt
Christmas Green	2068	Shirt, knee pads
Bright Red	2503	Leotards, face makeup, laces
White	2505	Shoes, face makeup
Navy Blue	2089	Shirt, shoes
Bright Yellow	2027	Socks
Pumpkin	2042	Bandana
Straw	2078	Rope, belt
Rainbow colors		Hair/wig

Flesh tones and eyes as in previous projects.

Finish with antiquing solution.

CHAPTER 9
Patterns and Line Drawings for Projects 1-15

Most of the project patterns in this section were originally carved from three inch basswood. There is nothing magical about three inch basswood. It just happens to be the size that is easiest for me to obtain and therefore I design most of my patterns to fit that dimension. You can easily reduce or enlarge these patterns if you have access to one of today's modern copy machines. I encourage you to modify, change or improve my patterns to suit your own needs or style. Build upon my original idea and make it better.

You don't have to be artistically inclined to develop your own patterns. My patterns begin with a crude sketch of my original idea. I use grid paper (4 squares to the inch) and a straight edge to create a front and side view. The grid paper helps to ensure that both views will match up evenly. This is the method I use to work out a pattern -- mainly trial and error with lots of erasures and re-adjustments.

The corresponding line drawings that accompany the bandsaw patterns are for detail reference and are not meant to be used as a pattern. These line drawings are by Herbert Kaminski of Crivitz, Wisconsin.

Pattern Index

		page
Project	01 Confused Cowboy	64
Project	02 Cowboy P. H. D.	66
Project	03 Rummy Belcher	68
Project	04 Ricky Wreck	70
Project	05 Cowboy Cowboy Carver	72
Project	06 Cowtown Santa	74
Project	07 Doc Croakum	76
Project	08 Digger Dirge	78
Project	09 Bronc-itis	80
Project	10 Shady Schyster	82
Project	11 Brother Paul	84
Project	12 Sage Soliloquy	86
Project	13 Bad Dude Bandit	88
Project	14 The Tailgater	90
Project	15 Slug Hazard	92

Many of these projects are available as duplicarved blanks from the author or from Rossiter's Ruffouts and Carving Supply, 1447 South Santa Fe, Wichita, Kansas 67211.
(Toll free 1-800-8-BLANKS)

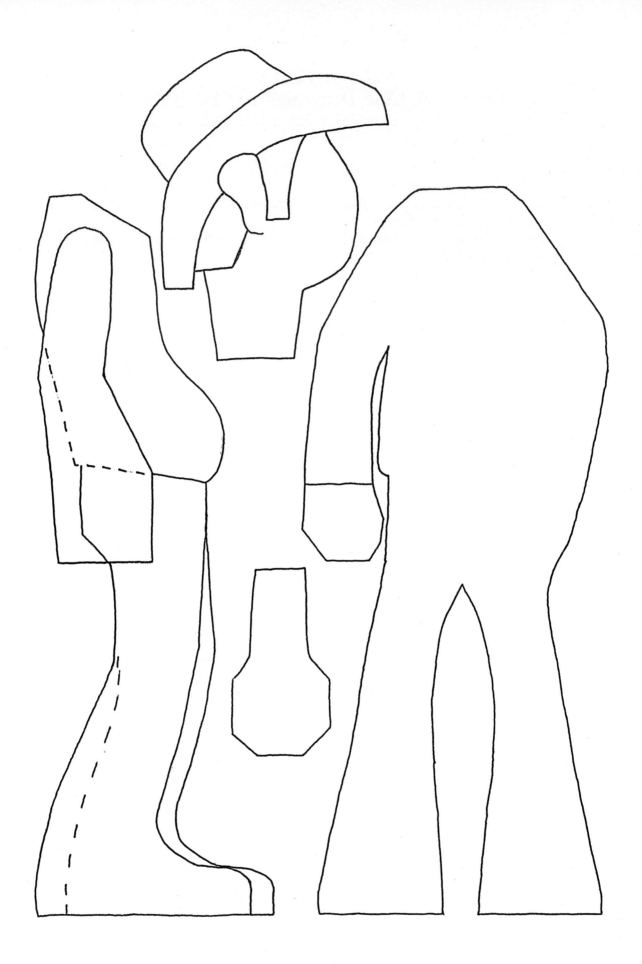

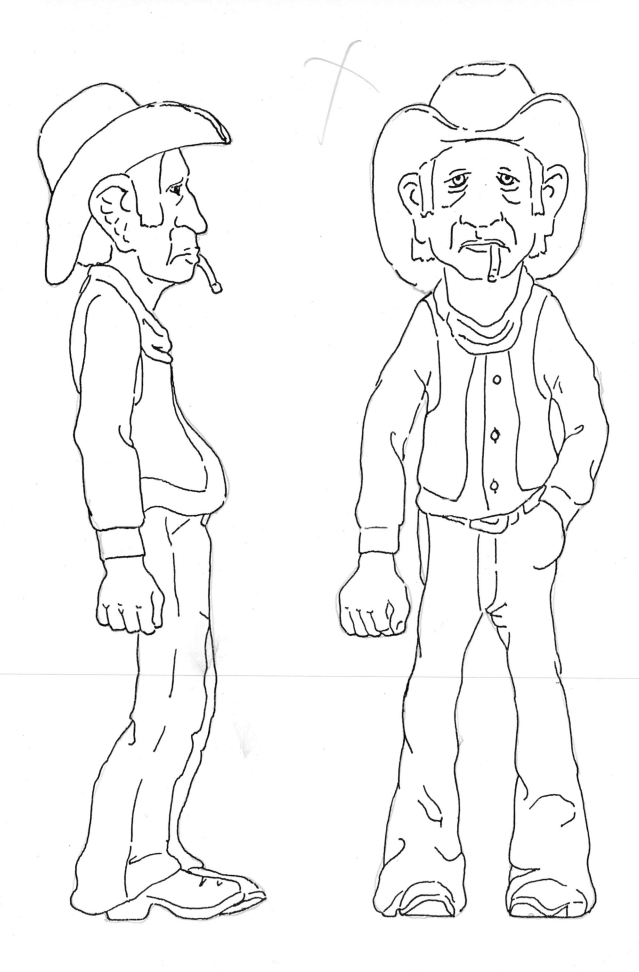

65

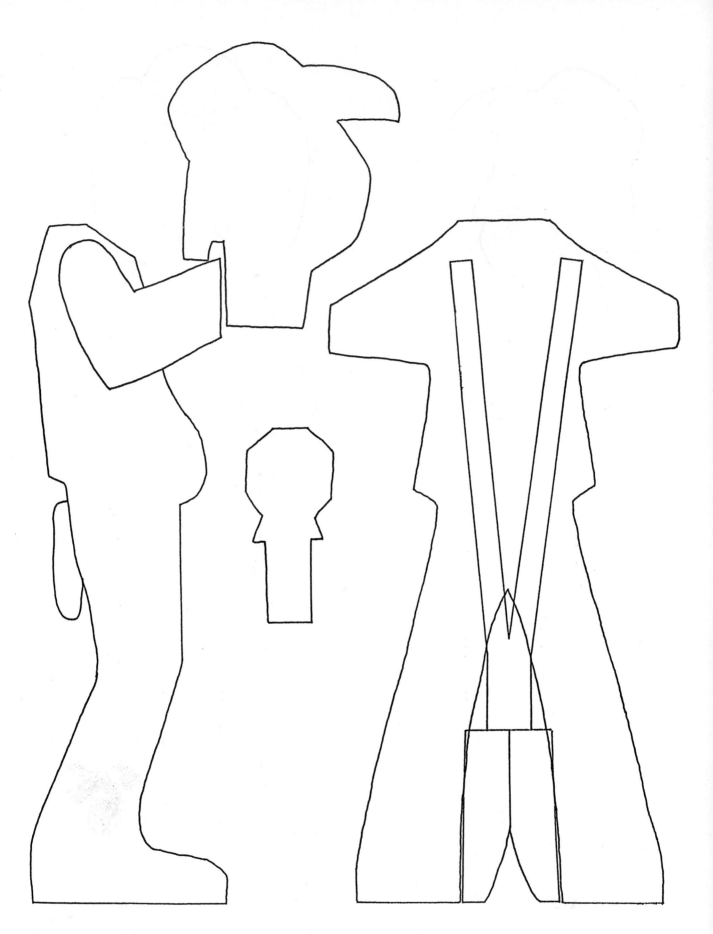

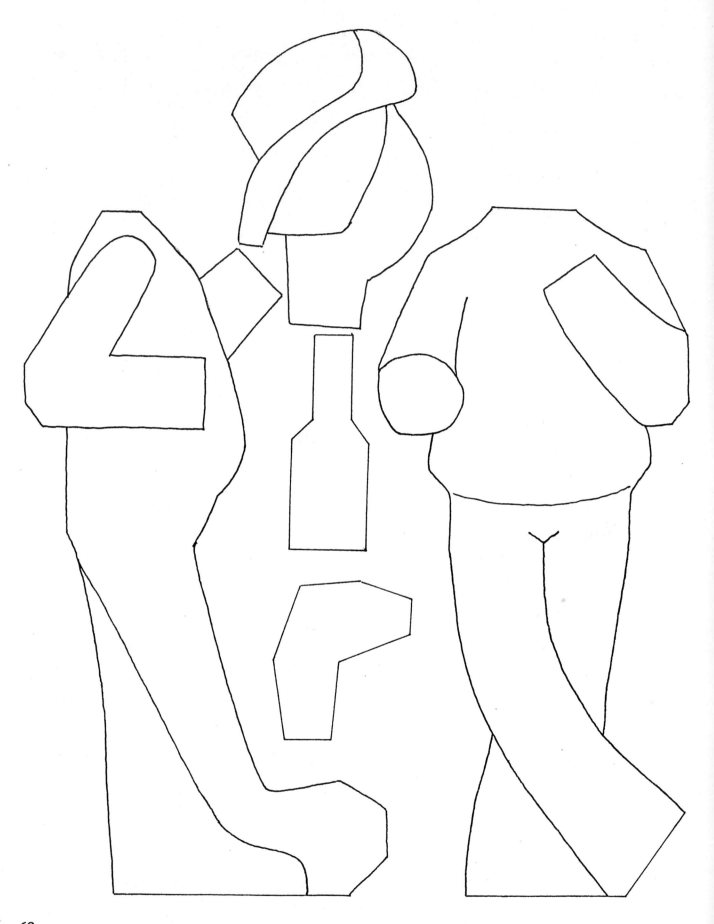

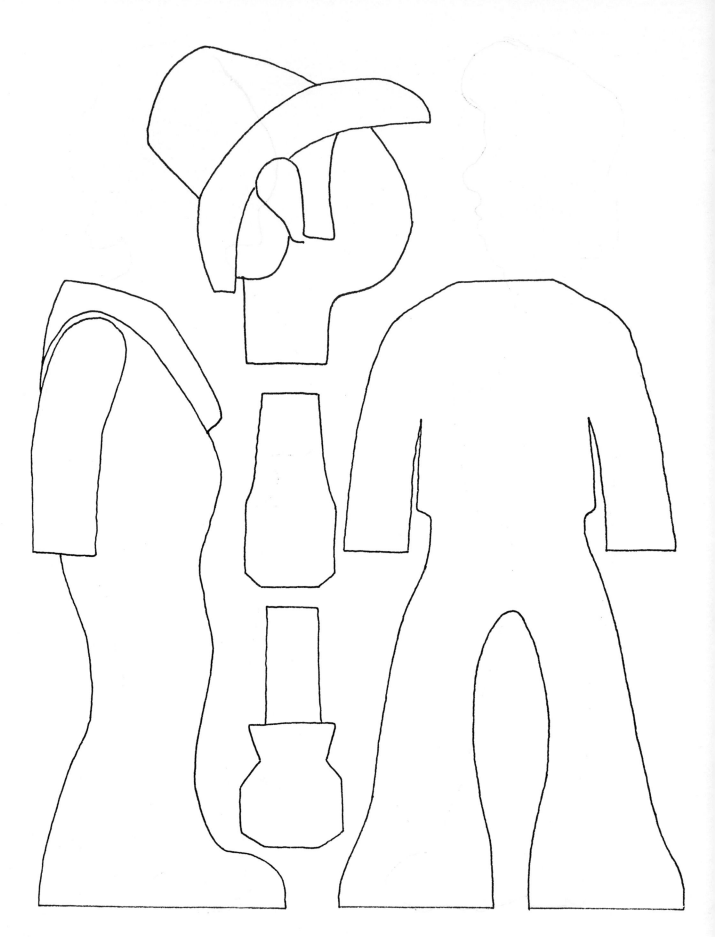

70

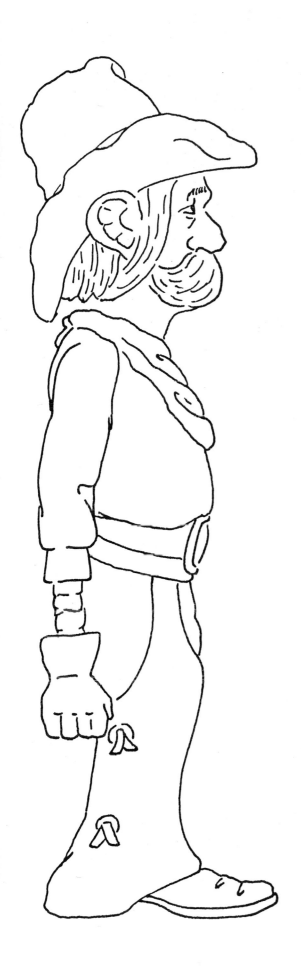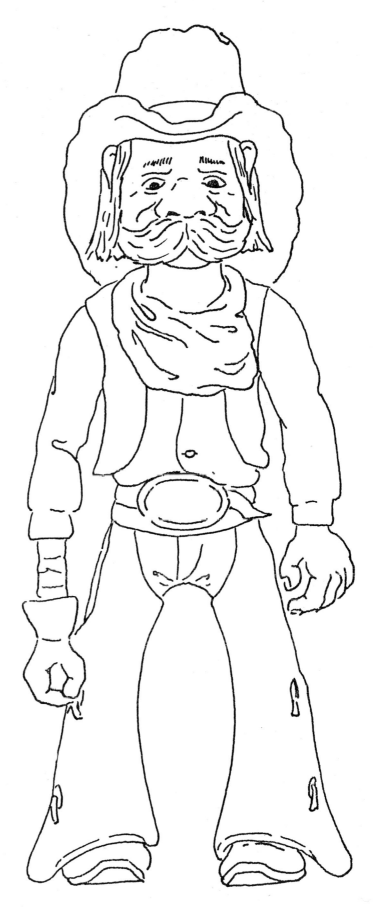

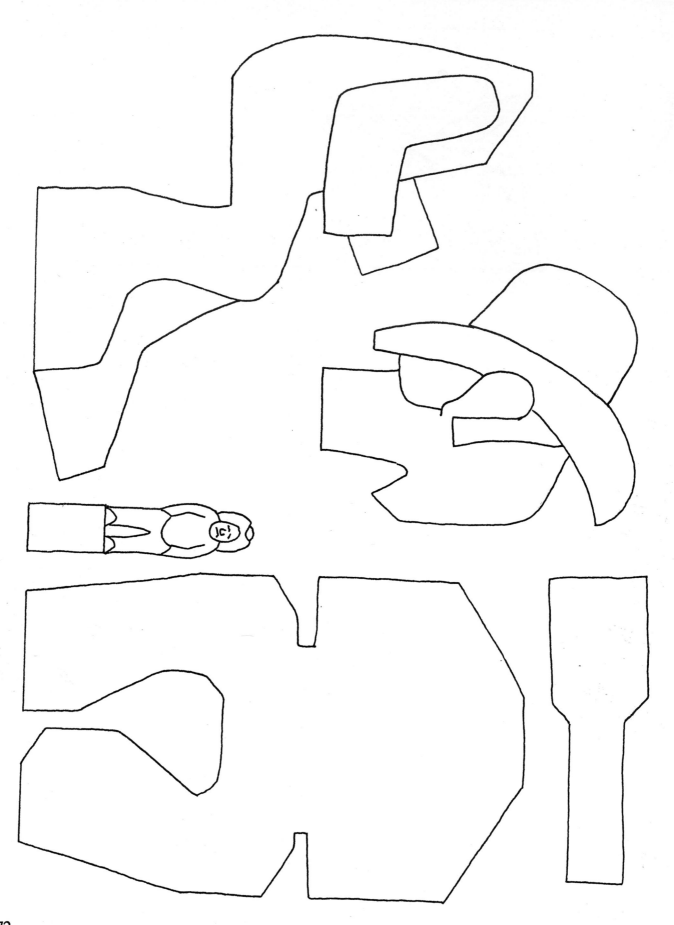

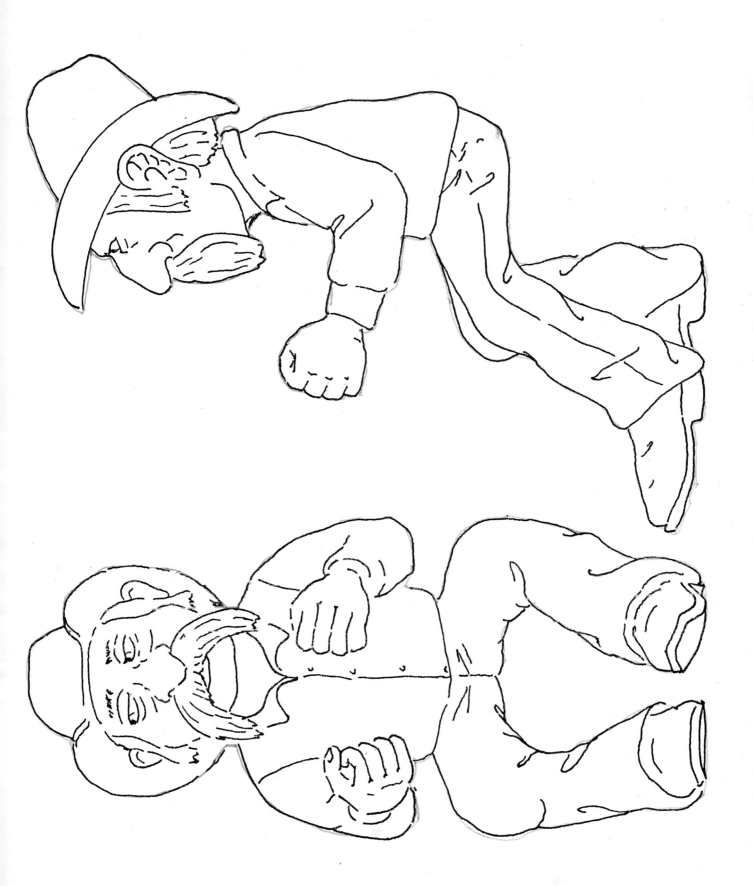

73

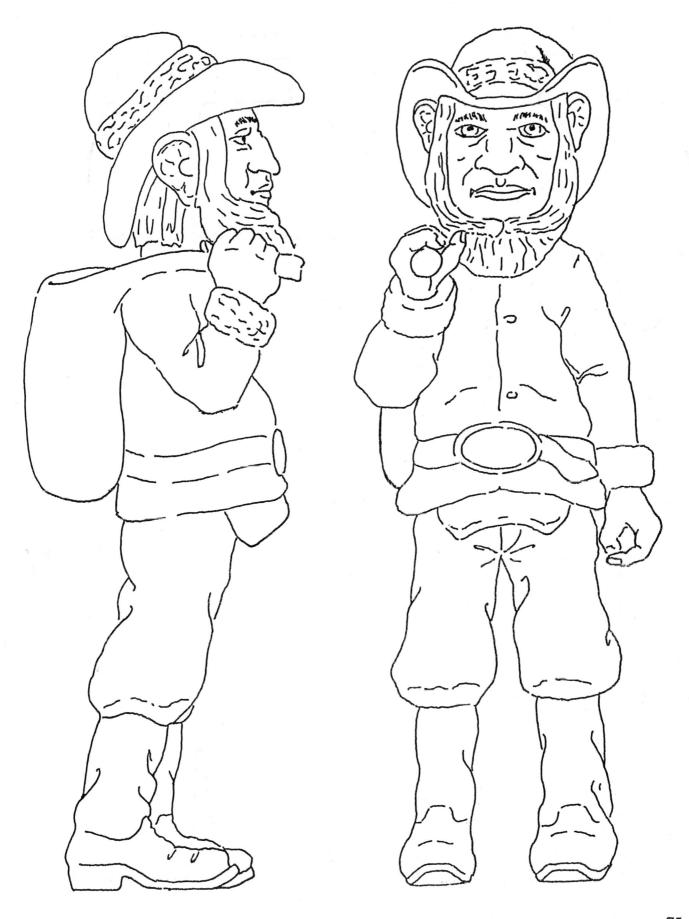

75

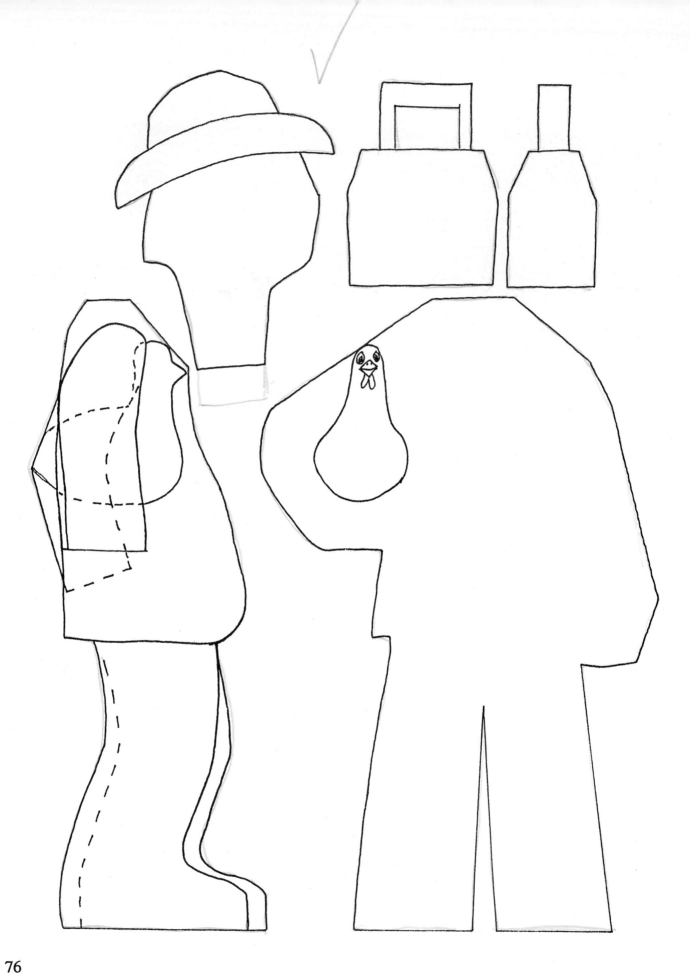

78

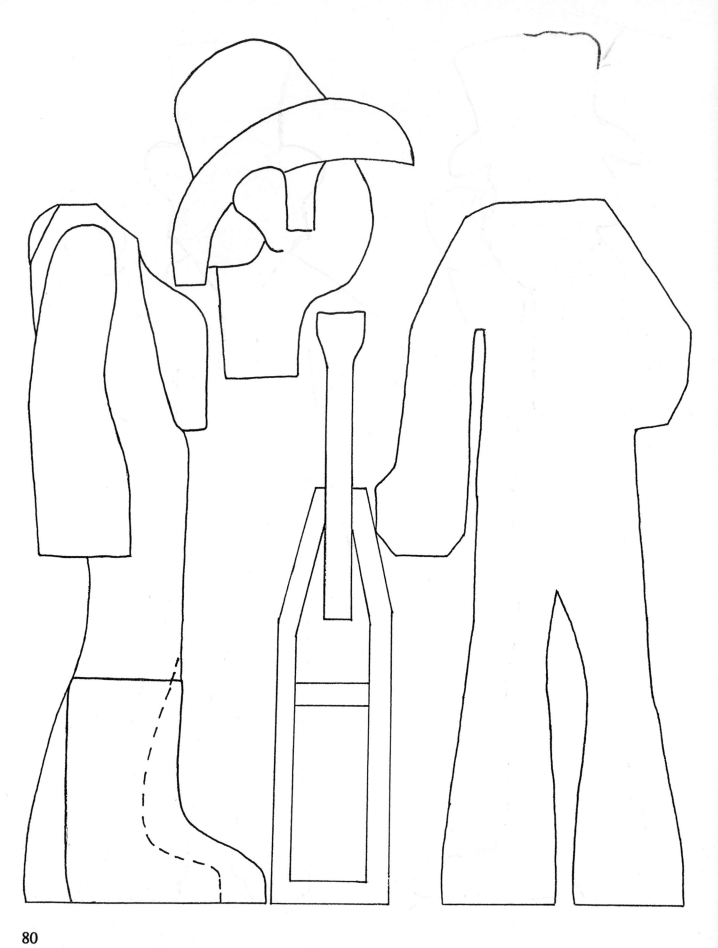

80

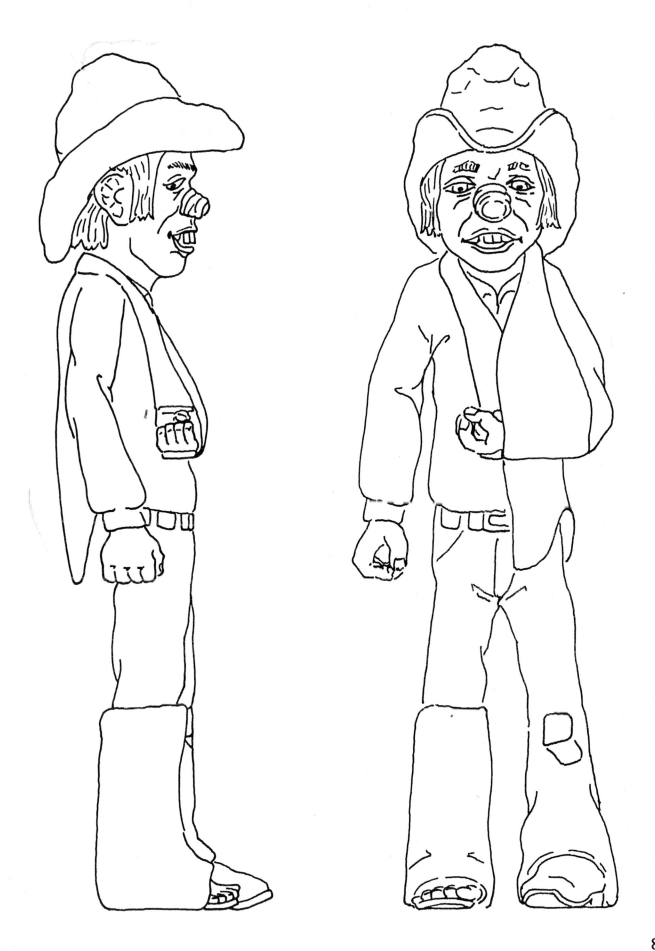

84

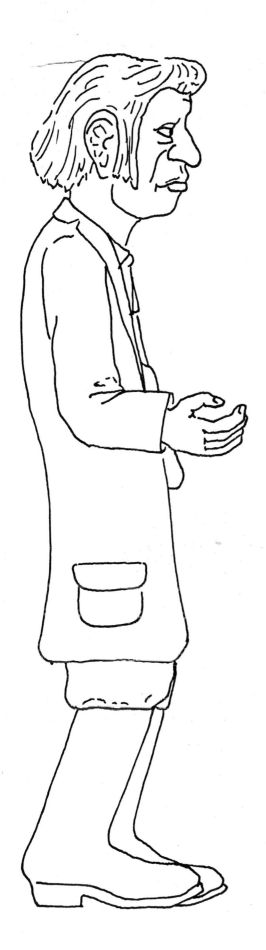

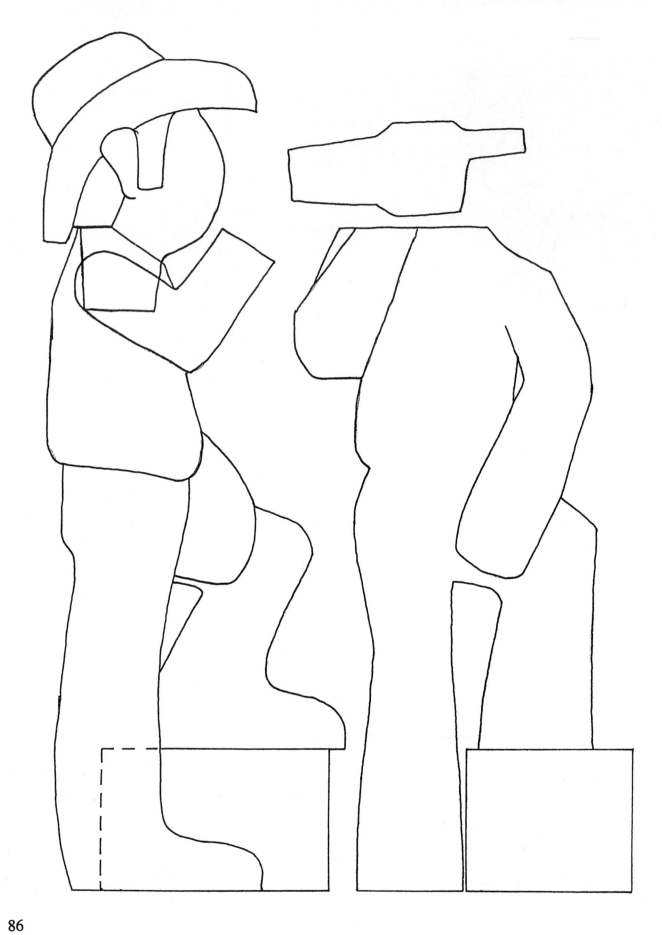

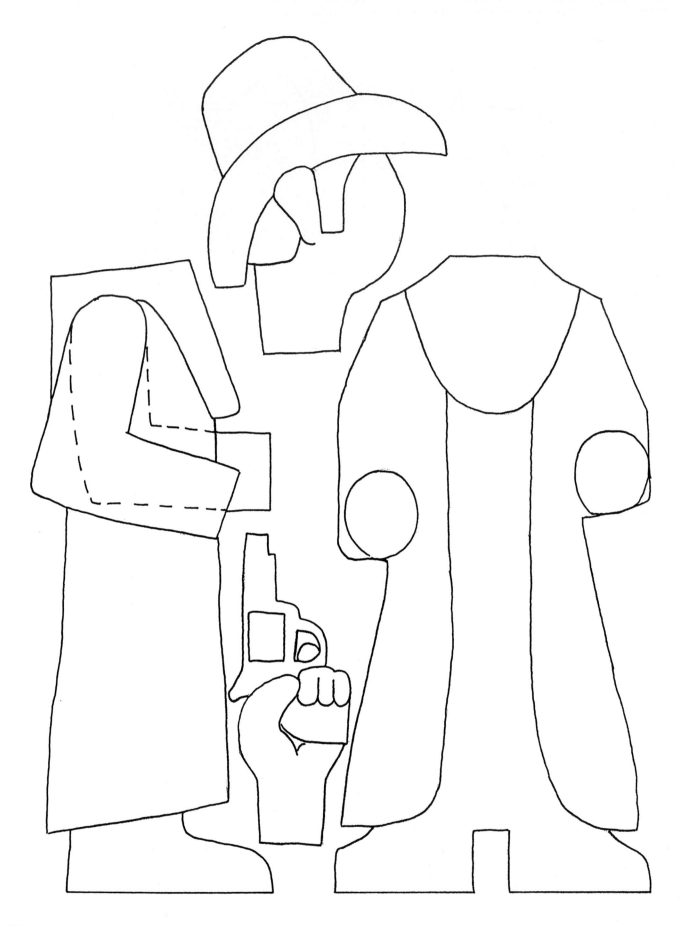

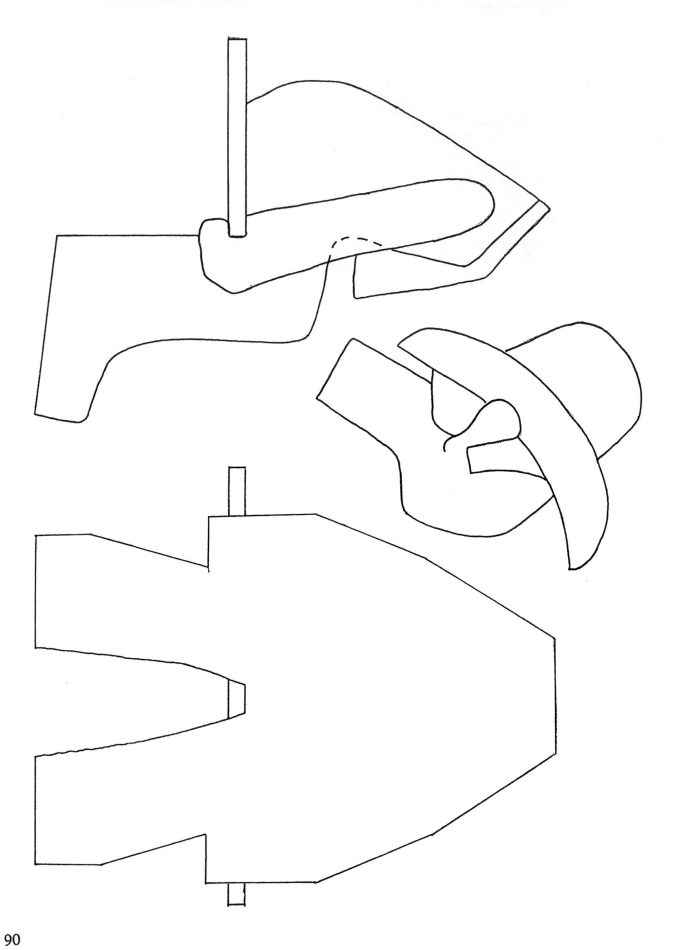

AFTERWORD

This book writing stuff is hard work. My hat is off to those of you who have done it before me. Carving is a lot easier taught one on one and explaining how to carve in written words is really tough. I hope that those of you who read my feeble attempts at authorship will be more gracious than I have been to other authors. I should have heeded my high school English teacher, Mrs. Meyers', admonition that indeed one day we would use all that writing nonsense that she tortured us with in school.

Revisions, rewrites, revisions, and more rewrites. There seems to be no end. Even with all that effort, I'm sure that you'll find plenty of mistakes that I've overlooked or ways that it could have been done better. I apologize in advance for my transgressions and omissions.

As I look back at what I've written, I realized that my educational background as a biology and physical education major are evident in my approach to design and carving. This text is very anatomically and kinesiologically oriented and I hope this approach interests and benefits you. I also found out that after writing chapters on faces, eyes, and hands that there isn't much to discuss for each project.

This has taken me about four years of work off and on. Would I do it again? Will I write another book? My first response is "No Way"! But on second thought, I have too much material not to write another book. Maybe I'll write one on animal caricature or sports figures, more cowboys, or maybe something really "off the wall".